# ROBERT MITCHUM

# ROBERT MITCHUM

*A Pyramid Illustrated History of the Movies*

**by**
**JOHN BELTON**

*General Editor:* **TED SENNETT**

**PUBLICATIONS**
**NEW YORK**

*To Ellen and Elizabeth*

**ROBERT MITCHUM**
**A Pyramid Illustrated History of the Movies**

Copyright © 1976 by Pyramid Communications, Inc.

Pyramid edition published April 1976

Library of Congress Catalog Card Number: 76-3340

Printed in the United States of America

Pyramid Books are published by Pyramid Publications (Harcourt Brace Jovanovich). Its trademarks, consisting of the word "Pyramid" and the portrayal of a pyramid, are registered in the United States Patent Office.

Pyramid Publications
(Harcourt Brace Jovanovich)
757 Third Avenue, New York, N.Y. 10017

Layout and graphic design by Anthony Basile

# ACKNOWLEDGMENTS

I would like to thank my wife Ellen and my friend Marty Lubin for their help in the preparation of this manuscript. I also want to thank Chris Baffer, Joseph Balian, Jeanine Basinger, Roger Ebert, Robert Edelstein, Robert Gitt, Tim Hunter, Peter Jaszi, Michael Moore, David Parker, Lee Saunders, Ted Sennett, Pat Sheehan, Alain Silver, Charles Silver, Anthony Slide, Eric Spilker, Jon Sonneborn, and Boris and Steve Zmijewsky.

*Photographs:* Jerry Vermilye, The Memory Shop, Cinemabilia, Movie Star News, and the companies that produced and distributed the films of Robert Mitchum.

# CONTENTS

Robert Mitchum is Hollywood's most durable non-conformist. His career is characterized by unconventional behavior both in the roles he plays and in his own lifestyle, making his success as a screen personality all the more surprising. Mitchum, though always an outsider working without recognition on the fringes of the motion picture industry, has beaten the system, preserving his integrity as an iconoclastic rebel. Yet he became and has remained a box office attraction.

Mitchum's survival as an anti-establishment figure reflects the peculiar nature of his subversiveness as a star. Lackadaisical and lethargic, he has outlived younger contemporaries like James Dean and Montgomery Clift whose inner torments surfaced in the characters they played, and whose real-life self-destructiveness was the working out of a cosmic kind of typecasting. The pent-up anger of a Dean, Clift, Brando, or Garfield has revolutionary overtones. Mitchum's screen persona, though seemingly complacent, is, in fact, anarchic. Characteristically unemotional, anti-materialistic, and disrespectful of authority, Mitchum appears not to care about anything. Beneath his superficial charm and wit lies a disturbing cynicism. *Photoplay* once called him "a seamy-sided idealist—a

# INTRODUCTION: BYRON WITH A BROKEN NOSE

cynic with a sentimental heart."

Yet Mitchum defies categorization. He exists independently of institutions, organizations and groups: he remains true only to himself, achieving an uncompromising integrity. "I've still got the same attitude I had when I started. I haven't changed anything but my underwear," he once told a *Time* interviewer in 1968. Although the remark referred to Mitchum's reaction to his success in films, it might easily have been made by any of the nonconformist characters he has played. Neither reformer nor revisionist, Mitchum is the quintessential nihilist. His energy has no direction; his desires have no object; his behavior is governed by no recognizable moral system. Robert Mitchum is Hollywood's foremost exponent of anomie.

Mitchum's anarchic nature, ideally suited to the cynical spirit of post-war America, undoubtedly accounts for his popularity in the late forties and early fifties. He was "beat" before the media created the beatnik, an itinerant before Kerouac and Kesey hit the road. His roles at RKO from 1944 to 1954 exploited these qualities: he

OUT OF THE PAST (1947). As Jeff

*WHERE DANGER LIVES*
(1950). As Jeff Cameron

played rootless, quasi-poetic loners who drifted around the world from adventure to adventure. In post-Vietnam, post-Watergate America, Mitchum's rebellious disaffection and weary patience reflect a contemporary loss of ideals.

In spite of his iconoclastic image—or perhaps because of it—Mitchum's appeal is broadly based. Audiences respond to the anti-authoritarian in his character without taking into account its chaotic consequences, just as the adventurous and romantic Mitchum character becomes involved in situations and with characters without knowing where they will lead him.

Mitchum's own life has been remarkably like those of the characters he plays in films. His biography reads like a picaresque novel: born in Bridgeport, Connecticut on August 6, 1917 and fatherless before the age of two, Mitchum spent his youth running away from home. One of the original Wild Boys of the Road, he quit the school he was attending in New York's "Hell's Kitchen" at fourteen and went on the road. He hitchhiked, rode freights and worked odd jobs, crossing the country in this way nine times. Mitchum says: "I worked in one-arm restaurants washing dishes and hauling slop, and, when I got to California, I lay on the beach and rolled drunks. I didn't know any better."

Arrested for vagrancy at the age of sixteen, he spent six days on a Georgia chain gang. According to Mitchum, "It was the Chatham County Camp No. 1, Pipemaker Swamp, in Savannah. They arrested me for what they called 'hanging around.' They put you in chains and whacked you around for laughs. The next time I was down there was to star in Cape Fear. In honor of the occasion, they ran my old mug shot on the front page of the local paper. They're great folks down there." Mitchum escaped before finishing his sentence. His life was a series of such Warner Bros. plots.

During the thirties, he worked as a stevedore, coal miner, ditch digger for the CCC, punch-press operator, night-club bouncer, prize-fighter (he got his nose broken) and adagio dancer. In 1936, his sister got him a job as a stage-hand at the Long Beach Civic Theatre. He played a few bit parts in The Petrified Forest, Remember the Day, and Rebound and began writing poetry and children's plays. Later, he began to write for a living. He wrote skits and composed bawdy songs for night-club acts. In 1939, he wrote an oratorio that was produced by Orson Welles and performed at the Hollywood Bowl. He wrote radio shows and ghost-wrote speeches and newspaper columns for Hollywood astrologer Carroll Righter. In 1940, he married his childhood sweetheart (Dorothy Spence) in Delaware and settled in California. He worked days at Lockheed Aircraft on a metal-shaping machine. At night, he appeared in small theater productions. At Lockheed he developed chronic insomnia (which he still suffers from) and began to lose his eyesight, apparently because he hated his job. The company doctor convinced him that he should quit. He eventually landed a small part in a Hopalong Cassidy film, replacing a cowboy who had been killed when a horse threw him. He was drafted in 1945, but was granted a dependency discharge eight months later. In 1945, he was cast as Captain Walker in William Wellman's *Story of G.I. Joe*. His performance earned him an Academy Award nomination as best supporting actor.

In 1948, Mitchum was arrested, along with some others, for possession of marijuana. He was found guilty and sentenced to sixty days on a work farm. When asked on his release what jail was like, he replied, "It's just like Palm Springs without the riff-raff." It was rumored that he had been framed by headline-hunting Los Angeles officials. In 1951, Mitchum's lawyer, Jerry Geisler (who successfully defended Charles Chaplin in a paternity suit and Errol Flynn in his rape case) won a review of the case. Mitchum's plea was changed to "not guilty," and his conviction was expunged from the records.

Mitchum makes no attempt to deny his past; in fact, he seems to consider it a crucial part of his screen identity. He repeatedly refers to his prison sentences in interviews and casts himself in semi-autobiographical parts: he has played ex-cons in *The Night of the Hunter* (1955), *Cape Fear* (1962), *Going Home* (1972) and *The Friends of Eddie Coyle* (1973), and in most of his films he has a questionable past. Mitchum's persona in interviews has become so fused with the parts he plays that it is almost impossible to distinguish the man from his movie roles. In a publicity release for *Bandido* (1956) in which he plays a wanderer and soldier-of-fortune, he wrote: "I've always led a kind of soldier-of-fortune life. I've done the things I want to do. I've had a lot of fun out of life, and a lot of life out of the fun in the world. I've been accused of many wild statements about my life, and some people tell me they can't decide where fiction leaves off and fact begins. Many of my statements have been smoke screens, designed to allow me to follow my own course without exposing it. I learned early in life that by telling a story more colorful than the truth, the truth would be let alone. I like to be let alone."

Like the anecdotes he tells, the parts Mitchum plays, though fictitious, reflect an underlying truth.

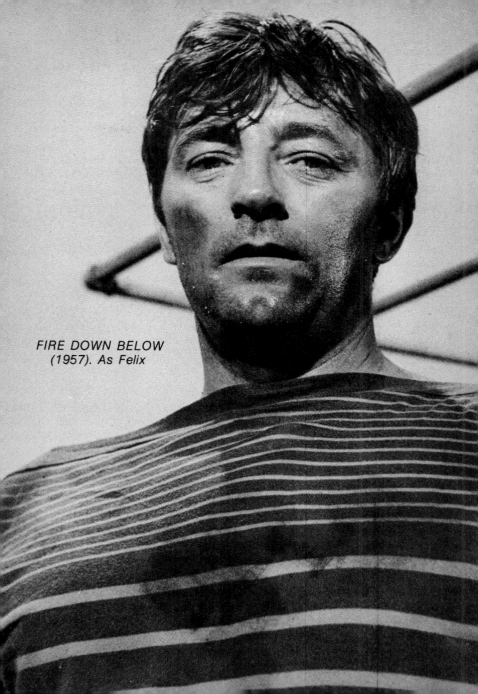

*FIRE DOWN BELOW*
*(1957). As Felix*

His screen persona grows out of his own experiences; as a result, he has a vitality and immediacy on the screen that many other actors lack. Method actors study acting in schools, analyze characters and invent experiences. Their approach to character is intellectual and, in a sense, artificial. Mitchum's acting is rooted in his own experiences. He learned about people in the street, in railway yards, on the road and in jail. He never analyzes or thinks through a character. His approach to character is essentially intuitive.

Mitchum's acting is physical and instinctive. He uses none of the tics, tricks or mannerisms that sophisticated audiences consider to be the accoutrements of the "real" actor. His performances lack dramatic rhetoric; they are built, instead, around more concrete elements: rhythms of movement and vocal nuance. Mitchum gets into character nakedly, without makeup or props. He rarely uses gesture. He acts, instead, with his voice, his eyes, his face and his body. Though Mitchum is commonly classified as an action star, he's as much a talker as he is a fighter, and, like Humphrey Bogart, he can handle witty dialogue as well as he can take a punch.

His voice is soft, low-pitched, mellow and romantic; in tone, it is similar to that of Bing Crosby, whom producers once thought Mitchum resembled. He sings, always in character, in a number of his films and has written and recorded several popular songs (including "Thunder Road"). He speaks with accents and regional dialects in more than a dozen films. He has won acclaim for his command of foreign accents in films like *The Sundowners* (1960) and *Ryan's Daughter* (1970), and his ear for American dialects, so evident in *The Night of the Hunter* (1955), *Heaven Knows, Mr. Allison* (1957), *Thunder Road* (1958) and *Home From the Hill* (1960), has been unjustly ignored.

Mitchum's eyes, like his voice, are romantic. They are also lazy and insolent. When he first looks at a woman—for example, at Jane Russell in *Macao* (1952)—his eyes undress her and rakishly explore her body; yet his look can also be tender and soft. He has been described as "sleepy-eyed"; perhaps his chronic insomnia contributes to this image. With characteristic irony, Mitchum caricatures himself: "They could never decide to their satisfaction what type I was. One would say, 'He's a broken-nosed Byronic.' Another would say, 'No, he ain't; he's an all-American boy.' People started talking about Mitchum-type roles, but I still don't know what they mean. They'd paint eyes on my eyelids, man, and I'd walk through it."*

* Mike Tomkies, *The Robert Mitchum Story*, New York: Ballantine Books, 1973, pp. 60-61.

Mitchum's face has the kind of flaws and fascinating contradictions that make an actor interesting to look at. It is handsome yet tough, sensual but sinister, strong yet vulnerable, profane but honest. It enables him to play romantic heroes and sleazy villains. One female fan described it as "the most immoral face I've ever seen." Mitchum himself maintains that he looks "like a shark with a broken nose." He says: "I became a leading man at a time when ugly leading men had become popular. People were tired . . . of the collar ad types. . . . After the war, suddenly there was this thing for ugly heroes, so I started going around in profile."

Mitchum's most distinctive features are his high cheekbones (his grandmother was a Blackfoot Indian), a dimpled chin which frequently causes foreigners to mistake him for Kirk Douglas, and a long upper lip that protrudes beyond his lower lip and gives his mouth a sensuous look. He is built like a Great American Bison: his massive head, shoulders and chest taper down to a narrow waist. Directors find him difficult to dress. Indeed, they prefer to undress him; he takes his shirt off in most of his films and his bare chest in movie ads still sells tickets. He walks with his back straight, moving with fluid co-ordination of his hips and shoulders. His gait—unlike, say, John Wayne's more purposeful stride—is insinuatingly languourous and indolent: it is as if he has nowhere in particular to go and is in no special hurry to get there.

Mitchum's physical attributes are decidedly American, a melting together of various ethnic characteristics into a combination that, like his voice, defies regional or ethnic classification. Though Mitchum is a classic American type, he remains unique among Hollywood actors. He conveys none of the youthful innocence of a Jimmy Stewart or the honest simplicity of a Gary Cooper—qualities that made these actors exceptional Frank Capra heroes. Admittedly, Stewart and Cooper changed after the war, both becoming more worldly, but even in his less innocent Hitchcock period, Stewart has an idealistic tenaciousness of purpose and obsessive determination that Mitchum lacks. And though Cooper loses his sense of humor and his idealism becomes tinged with bitterness in films like *The Fountainhead* (1949) or *High Noon* (1952), his strength retains a moral integrity that Mitchum, eternally vulnerable, can never achieve. Where John Wayne's active strength conveys a moral infallibility, Mitchum's power is undercut by an inner sloth or laziness. His inertia repeatedly gets him into trouble, and he is constantly plagued by his own mistakes.

Wayne has to climb down from Mt. Rushmore to become human. Mitchum's climb is always upward: he is forever mortal.

Mitchum, like James Cagney, generally plays lower- or middle-class characters. He has Cagney's toughness, but the quality of his toughness is different. Cagney conveys the cockiness and aggressiveness of a first-generation Irish immigrant; his energy is channelled toward "making it." Whereas Cagney's reach often exceeds his grasp, Mitchum keeps his hands in his own pockets; he remains apathetic to the material and social goals that motivate Cagney.

Mitchum is lower-class and earthy; he has common sense and his feet are firmly planted on the ground. Yet he is always falling for a phony sob story, irrationally getting involved in other people's troubles. As if bored with himself and his own affairs, he courts new experiences for their own sake. A post-war adventurer, he lacks Errol Flynn's grace, polish and inflated sense of self—qualities which properly belong to an earlier era. Where Mitchum's modernity prevents him from playing swashbucklers, Flynn's anachronistic talents, combined with his lower-class aspirations to nobility, make him ideal for period pictures like *Gentleman Jim* (1942).

The actor Mitchum most closely resembles is Humphrey Bogart. They share the same rough good looks and the same moral ambiguity. Both can play good guys and bad guys with equal facility, and both also create unsympathetic heroes and sympathetic villains.

Mitchum and Bogart are Hollywood's greatest romantic cynics. Warily distrustful yet blindly passionate, they fall victim to their own contradictory feelings toward women. Both are archetypal forties *film noir* lovers; Bogart in *The Maltese Falcon* (1941) and Mitchum in *Out of the Past* (1947) play skeptical detectives who fall for fascinatingly beautiful, corrupt and corrupting women. Characteristically, Bogart, more in control of his feelings than Mitchum and shrewder than his female adversary, extricates himself at the last minute while Mitchum, rarely the master of his own emotions and usually one step behind his opponents, sticks around a bit longer than he should, held as much by his curiosity as his laziness, and fails to free himself from an impossible tangle of passion and plot. Bogart's cynicism holds his romanticism in check: his wits enable him to survive. Mitchum lives by his instincts rather than by his intellect and, more often than not, destroys himself.

As a lover, Mitchum is sexy but unemotional and passive. He rarely pursues his leading lady, even in films like *Rachel and the Stranger*

18

*THE LONGEST DAY (1962). As Brig. General Norman Cota*

GOING HOME (1972). As Harry Graham

(1948), *Holiday Affair* (1949) and *Rampage* (1963), where he announces that he will. He underplays love scenes, continually holding back his feelings. His masculine suppression of sentiment and affection suggests to women a potential for passion which they then try to help him realize. Women respond to his inscrutability; their attempts to possess or know him, however, invariably fail. He remains enigmatic and lonely.

Part of Mitchum's attraction lies in the poetic nature of his isolation. He is a self-willed outsider who views the world from an ironic distance. A modern-day troubadour, he wanders from place to place, from experience to experience, from woman to woman, sensing the world around him. What Dwight Whitney observes about the real-life Mitchum is equally true of the screen Mitchum: there is the "suggestion, implicit in every utterance, that within the body of this 'movie star' lies imprisoned the soul of a poet."*

Like the heroes in the Conrad novels he admires, Mitchum is a lonely adventurer, victimized by his own irrational impulses and by the chaotic forces in the world around him. Mitchum never anguishes over his actions as Conrad's heroes do, nor are his obsessions as all-consuming; but like them, he carries a great mystery within him. It is this elusiveness that makes him one of the most interesting and most baffling of American actors.

* TV Guide, June 7, 1969

After leaving his job at Lockheed and a short stint as a shoe salesman, Mitchum began to look for acting jobs in films. Booking agent Jack Shay got him an interview with Harry Sherman, producer of the popular Hopalong Cassidy series that had recently moved to United Artists from Paramount. Sherman asked Mitchum whether he could ride a horse, and Mitchum gave him a story about once being a cowboy in Laredo. Mitchum says: "I got a part in a Hopalong Cassidy picture. The old timers knew I was a greenhorn, so the first thing that happened in my screen debut was this: some wise guy palmed a trick horse off on me. I clambered aboard for my first scene and the nag threw me about forty feet." The film was *Hoppy Serves a Writ* (1943), and Mitchum was thrown three times before he mastered the horse. Mitchum, stuntman and extra, played one member of a gang of rustlers lured out of wide-open Oklahoma Territory into Texas, where sheriff Cassidy arrests them. He was now a professional actor, earning "fifty dollars a week and all the hay I could eat."

Bit parts followed in *The Leather Burners* (1943), *Border Patrol* (1943) and *Colt Comrades* (1943). In *Border Patrol* he played a gunslinger for a crooked mine owner, and in *Colt Comrades* a desperado on the wrong side of a range war over water rights. Mitchum won

# $50 A WEEK AND ALL THE HAY I COULD EAT

small roles in *Follow the Band* (1943), a Universal musical studded with specialty acts; in *The Human Comedy* (1943), as one of three soldiers who meet small town girls during a weekend furlough and in *We've Never Been Licked* (1943), a wartime film set at Texas A & M. Mitchum won favorable notices as a hazing upperclassman on the periphery of a conspiracy that dealt with secret formulas and Japanese espionage.

Mitchum's first big role was that of Trigger Dolan in Republic's *Beyond the Last Frontier* (1943), where he helps an undercover Texas Ranger bring to justice the gang to which he belongs. In *Bar 20* (1943), another Cassidy oater, he became a good guy, a rancher trying to recover jewels stolen from his girlfriend. By now, Mitchum was established in his profession. He was getting "a hundred bucks a week and all the horse manure I could take home."

In *Doughboys in Ireland* (1943), a musical war film, Mitchum played an American G.I. stationed in Ireland during the war. In *Corvette K-225* (1943), he had a very small part as a sailor on a lightly armed Canadian destroyer

*HOPPY SERVES A WRIT (1943). With William Boyd*

escort. In *False Colors* (1943) and *Riders of the Deadline* (1943), Mitchum, again playing villains, made his final appearances in the Cassidy series. "I was now a character actor, and I played just about everything," Mitchum quips, "Chinese laundrymen, midgets, Irish washerwomen, faggots. I even played a journalist once."

In *The Dancing Masters* (1943), Mitchum has two walk-ons as Mickey, a racketeer's henchman who sells "protection" and phony insurance to Laurel and Hardy, operators of a bankrupt dancing

school. Mitchum's manner is intimidating, especially when he slowly pushes his hat back on his head and stares icily at Stan and Ollie's secretary. Eager to do well in this Fox production, Mitchum came on strong, aggressively taking charge of the scenes he was in.

Walter Wanger's *Gung Ho!* (1943) is a propagandistic recruitment film about the creation of a special Green Beret-type raider batallion which becomes instrumental in the taking of Maikin Island in the Pacific. Mitchum, the archetypal dogface, plays a charac-

*WE'VE NEVER BEEN LICKED (1943). With Richard Quine (holding Japanese money)*

*DOUGHBOYS IN IRELAND (1943). Mitchum is third from the left.*

*THE DANCING MASTERS (1943). With George Lloyd, Oliver Hardy, and Stan Laurel*

ter called "Pig Iron." A former farm boy, he has been in the brig four times since joining the army. When Randolph Scott interviews him for the outfit, Mitchum's replies to Scott's questions are simple, direct and honest. His pig-iron toughness has integrity; he is obviously not the buffoon that the other volunteers seem to be.

Leading an attack after his sergeant is shot, Mitchum gets wounded in the throat. Recuperating back at camp, he spots a Japanese about to kill an American doctor. Unable to shout a warning, he throws his knife, kills the Jap, and falls back exhausted onto his stretcher. *Gung Ho*, Chinese for "work on to-gether," connotes enthusiasm, loyalty and *esprit de corps*. Mitchum, characteristically energetic in his early film roles, is *gung ho.*

*Johnny Doesn't Live Here Anymore* (1944), a romantic comedy about the problems of wartime living, was re-released as *And So They Were Married* largely to capitalize on Mitchum's subsequent popularity. He appears only in the last reel, playing one of the eleven soldiers given keys to an apartment unwittingly sublet by Simone Simon.

*When Strangers Marry* (1944), later re-released as *Betrayed*, is generally regarded as one of the best "B" films ever made. Praised

JOHNNY DOESN'T LIVE HERE ANY MORE (1944). With
James Ellison and William Terry

WHEN STRANGERS MARRY (1944). With Kim Hunter

*THIRTY SECONDS OVER TOKYO (1944). With Van Johnson*

by Orson Welles and by critics James Agee and Manny Farber, the film, according to Farber's *New Republic* review, captures "the solemn melancholia of being troubled and lonely in a strange city." Shot in seven days by director William Castle, at a cost of $50,000, this murder mystery deals with the attempts of a bride to find her new husband, whom she suspects of murder. Mitchum, the real murderer and her former suitor, pretends to help her. *Variety* admired Mitchum's "breezy quality", and Farber praised his "sardonic, cold-faced" performance.

Director Mervyn LeRoy, who couldn't decide whether Mitchum was "the lousiest actor in the world or the best," cast him as one of the crew members of a B-25 that bombed Japan in *Thirty Seconds Over Tokyo* (1944). Mitchum's natural, relaxed and unpretentious presence here and in *When Strangers Marry* won him a long-term contract at RKO. He took a salary cut from $1000 to $350 a week, but the work was regular and he no longer had to scramble for jobs.

Mitchum's screen persona was not created or shaped by his directors. Dietrich had Sternberg, Wayne had Ford and Hawks, Stewart had Capra and Hitchcock. Rarely working with a director more than twice, Mitchum, like Bogart, created his own character. He did this partly with RKO's help and partly in spite of its hindrance. Charles Koerner, the man who fired Orson Welles, hired Mitchum and cast him unimaginatively in Zane Grey westerns. Koerner reformed Mitchum from outlaw to hero but did little else to change his cowboy image. Dore Schary injected literary class and social consciousness into the RKO product after Koerner's death in 1946; he beefed up RKO scripts with psychological concerns, setting a postwar trend for other studios to follow. To an extent, this rubbed off on Mitchum; the characters he played in *Till the End of Time* (1946), *Rachel and the Stranger* (1948) and the Schary-inspired *Blood on the Moon* (1948) became more complex. Mitchum's final transformation at RKO was under the aegis of Howard Hughes, head of the studio from 1948 to 1955. Hughes coarsened the studio's image (and Mitchum's), replacing its former intellectuality with a combination of vulgarity, exoticism and eroticism (personified by Jane Russell in her films with Mitchum). Before Hughes put RKO out of

# RKO'S MALE JANE RUSSELL

business, he masterminded Mitchum's transformation into a male Jane Russell: tough, wisecracking, and non-conformist, Mitchum began to live out of suitcases in out-of-the-way places like Mexico City, Acapulco and Macao.

Mitchum became RKO's workhorse and its last big star. He jokes about his tenure there: "RKO made the same film with me in it for ten years. They were so alike I wore the same suit in six of them and the same Burberry trench coat. They made a male Jane Russell out of me. I was the staff hero. They got so they wanted me to take some of my clothes off in the pictures. I objected to this, so I put on some weight and looked like a Bulgarian wrestler when I took my shirt off. Only two pictures I made in that time made any sense whatever. I complained and they told me frankly that they had a certain amount of baloney to sell and I was the boy to do it."[*]

Mitchum belittles his years at RKO, but they mark his emergence as a major star and his development into an accomplished actor. Although he began at rock bottom with *The Girl Rush* (1944), re-

[*] Interview with Don Ross, New York *Herald*, October 25, 1955.

29

*Early in his career*

markable only in that it includes Mitchum's first—and last—appearance in drag, and finished his term at the studio with *She Couldn't Say No* (1954), an empty-headed, pleasant comedy about philanthropy, there were some remarkable pictures and performances in between, including *Out of the Past, His Kind of Woman* (1951), *Macao, The Lusty Men* (1952) and *Angel Face* (1952). It was at RKO that Mitchum's screen image had begun to take shape, and by the time he left the studio in 1954, it was fully formed.

In *The Girl Rush*, a group of forty-niners imports a company of showgirls from San Francisco. Mitchum, straight man for comedy stars Wally Brown and Alan Carney, plays a young, rough-and-ready, yet soft-spoken prospector who escorts the girls and their two managers to town. In order to get the troupe into town without being shot by the crooked gambling hall owner, the men disguise themselves as women. Wearing a big smile, a blond wig and a gingham dress, Mitchum throws himself into his part, adjusting his wig, hitching up his pants beneath his dress, and batting his eyes at a tall prospector who tries to pick him up. Somehow Mitchum survives this business with his dignity intact, but it is clear from *The Girl Rush* that RKO had as yet no idea of what to do with their new star.

Mitchum is much better cast in Zane Grey's *Nevada* (1944) and *West of the Pecos* (1945). In these remakes of earlier Richard Dix programmers, Mitchum captures the primitive, diamond-in-the-rough quality of Grey's heroes. The Mitchum identity, however, is still in limbo. His youthful look, his long, lean, hard body and his sharp features belong to an earlier, more innocent era. As Jim Lacey in *Nevada*, Mitchum is framed for a murder by claim jumpers and narrowly rescued from a lynching by his friends. A bit unsure of himself and uncomfortable with the character he plays, Mitchum's performance here is full of pure, unchannelled, boyish vitality; yet it has a nervous, serious quality as well.

In *West of the Pecos*, Mitchum appears more comfortable with his character. Pecos Smith, an itinerant cowboy who lives outside the law, gives Mitchum the opportunity to play someone closer to himself. The brotherly and good-natured Smith guides a Chicago meatpacker and his daughter (dressed as a boy) through the lawless country west of the Pecos to their ranch. Mitchum's performance is bare, unassuming, controlled and understated. Though still full of energy, his style has become smoother and less tense.

It took an outsider, William Wellman, and an independent pro-

THE GIRL RUSH (1944). With Paul Newlin

WEST OF THE PECOS (1945). With Barbara Hale and Thurston Hall

THE STORY OF G.I. JOE (1945). As Lieutenant Walker

duction released through United Artists to reveal what RKO had not seen in Mitchum. With *The Story of G.I. Joe* (1945), Mitchum became an immediate star. Wellman and producer Lester Cowan cast him as Lieutenant Walker, the reflective, lonely, stony-faced officer of Company C—the platoon immortalized by war correspondent Ernie Pyle. The film's low-key narrative is built around the experiences of the common, dogface soldier. It conveys a feeling for army routine—getting in and out of convoy trucks, crossing rivers, marching in the rain, fighting unseen enemies in demolished churches. Wellman's populist concern for the ordinary guy and Pyle's human-interest approach to combat result in a realistic, yet poetic view of the infantryman's unheroic, unglamorous life during a war.

As an officer, Mitchum stands apart from his men, watching over them, writing letters to their families after they die, and breaking in their replacements. Mitchum, with a stubbly beard and a long, lean face, looks exhausted throughout the film, and his dramatically expressive eyes reflect an inner exhaustion, especially in those privileged moments when he tells Burgess Meredith, as Pyle, about his wife who walked out on

THE STORY OF G.I. JOE (1945). With Freddie Steele

him, or wonders philosophically about the war's misuse of human energy.

Mitchum says very little in the film; he acts, instead, with his eyes, blinking reflectively, helplessly watching one of his men go mad, or sadly sharing, through a glance, Meredith's first encounter with death. Andrew Sarris describes Mitchum's performance as "extraordinarily haunting." He writes: "Even after Freddie Steele's spine-tingling crack-up, Mitchum provides the emotional and metaphysical climax of the movie simply by being slung over a mule as a corpse, and led down the hill to the periphery of his platoon, and there

in death dangling in silent communion with his living comrades. It is an acting-out of one of the late Ernie Pyle's most eloquent journalistic insights into the ineffable link between the living and the dead, but I can't think of another actor who could have conveyed Mitchum's stately calm in this very dangerously narcissistic maneuver. The scene is still a convulsive emotional experience not because of any lingering idolatry of a dead G.I., but because Mitchum's exquisite stillness in death is the result of his expressive stoicism in life."*

Mitchum was drafted into the

* *Village Voice*, July 26, 1973.

34

*TILL THE END OF TIME (1946). As Bill Tabeshaw*

army during the shooting of *The Story of G.I. Joe*, but his induction was delayed until the film was completed. General Eisenhower praised the movie, and Mitchum was sent by the army to attend premieres of the film around the country. Demoted from sergeant to private several times, the real-life Mitchum was a reluctant soldier who had difficulty adjusting to army discipline. "When they took me away," he says, "I still had bits of the porch rails under my finger nails." Eight months after his induction, he was granted a dependency discharge as sole support of his mother, step-father, step-sister, wife and two sons.

Mitchum's success in *The Story of G.I. Joe* led to a renegotiation of his contract. Half of the contract was owned jointly by RKO and Howard Hughes; the other half was now picked up by David O. Selznick. Selznick lent Mitchum out to others but never used him himself, probably thinking that the actor was not classy or polished enough for his "prestige" films. The result was that RKO finally started giving Mitchum parts he could play.

Dore Schary now took charge of Mitchum, casting him as a returning war veteran in *Till the End of Time* (1946). Like William Wyler's *The Best Years of Our Lives* (1946), the film deals, though less

*UNDERCURRENT (1946). With Katharine Hepburn*

pretentiously, with the problems faced by soldiers returning to civilian life. Mitchum plays Bill Tabeshaw, winner of a silver star and purple heart. His war wounds are as much psychological as physical. He carries a silver plate in his head and cynicism in his heart. Tapping on his head, he jokes about his post-war prospects after he is mustered out: "With this hunk of silver and a real dime, I can always get a cup of coffee."

Mitchum drifts around after his release, full of purposeless energy and in no rush to go home. Like his war buddies, he is a "dead head, a piece of timber that has been waterlogged, that just sits and goes nowhere." But Mitchum has more vitality than his friends. He finally returns to Stinking Creek, New Mexico, to reclaim his old job as rodeo bronco buster. Later in the picture, he turns up unshaven and down on his luck, plagued by painful headaches caused by a fall from a horse. He borrows twenty dollars from war buddy Guy Madison in order to get drunk and relieve the pressure in his skull. After he is knocked unconscious in a brutal barroom brawl, an operation saves his life and relieves the pressure on his brain.

Mitchum's part was small. "All they wanted me to do," he says, "was stand there and point at the leading ladies while they wheeled them through." But with his cheerful cynicism, idiosyncratic behavior, and worldly self-awareness, he stands out against a more conventionally despondent cast of neurotics.

Characteristically, MGM misused Mitchum, on loan-out from RKO through Selznick, in a pair of turgid melodramas, *Undercurrent* (1946) and *Desire Me* (1947). RKO and Selznick (who got $25,000 a week for each MGM Mitchum picture and paid the actor $350 a week) ran Mitchum ragged. "I worked three pictures for twenty-six days straight," he remembers. "We'd shoot all night at RKO (*The Locket*), then I'd report for *Undercurrent* from seven in the morning until noon, when I'd be flown to Monterey to work all afternoon on the picture with Greer Garson (*Desire Me*)."

In Vincente Minnelli's *Undercurrent*, Mitchum, trying out his Bing Crosby look, plays a sensitive half-brother of industrialist Robert Taylor. Katharine Hepburn, Taylor's new wife, becomes curious about the missing Mitchum, whom she has never seen, and suspects he has met with foul play. Mitchum plays, against type, a serene, gentle character, interested in music, literature and art. Taylor, the psychopathic husband, tries—but fails—to kill Hepburn, and it is implied she turns to Mitchum.

Hepburn gave Mitchum a hard time, but the contrast between her highbrow, theatrical sense of acting and his natural, underplayed style provided an interesting counterpoint. During the making of the picture, Hepburn told him: "You know you can't act, and if you hadn't been good-looking you would never have gotten a picture. I'm tired of playing with people who have nothing to offer." What Mitchum had to offer was restraint and understatement, virtues that Hepburn and critics fond of stage histrionics have misinterpreted as unexpressiveness and lack of talent.

Mitchum has a small role in *Desire Me* as a French prisoner of war in a German concentration camp. During one of his several attempts at escape, he flees with comrade Richard Hart but is wounded and left for dead. He returns at the end of the film to reclaim his wife (Greer Garson) and house, both of which Hart has usurped. MGM kept rewriting the script during the production, bewildering the actors and losing director George Cukor, who was replaced by Mervyn LeRoy. Mitchum, obviously miscast, is only a peripheral figure in a film that properly belongs to Garson and Hart.

*The Locket* (1946), a pseudo-Freudian study of a schizophrenic kleptomaniac, has a remarkably complicated narrative structure, built around flashbacks within

*DESIRE ME (1947). With Greer Garson*

THE LOCKET (1946). With Laraine Day

flashbacks, that suits the convoluted relationships among the various characters in the film. Mitchum, cast in a small part as an abrasive, iconoclastic artist who berates his students and insults potential patrons, narrates one of the flashbacks to psychiatrist Brian Aherne. Mitchum suspects Aherne's wife (Laraine Day), a former art student and girlfriend, of stealing a valuable necklace, murdering its owner, and silently standing by while an innocent man is convicted of her crimes. Mitchum relates all this with a detached, unemotional calmness—outstanding traits in a film whose characters are victims of their own irrational passions—but he fails to convince Aherne that he is telling the truth. Mitchum's cynicism, as he confronts Day later at Aherne's apartment, masks deeper feelings of guilt over his complicity in the affair. (His love for Day has kept him from telling his suspicions to the police.) The next day, after the innocent man has been executed, Mitchum pays a final visit to Aherne's office, transfers his guilt to Aherne, and then jumps out of the psychiatrist's window to his death. Although many of the film's critics consider his suicide unconvincing, *The Locket*'s melancholy tone brings out latent obsessive traits in Mitchum as a moody and idealistic artist who refuses to compromise.

Similar in plot and theme to Selznick's *Duel in the Sun* (1946), *Pursued* (1947), also written by Niven Busch, was publicized as the first psychological western. Mitchum, on loan to Warners through Selznick, gives his first fully mature performance as Jeb Rand, a man tormented by strange nightmares and obsessed with discovering his origins. The film, directed by Raoul Walsh, is told in flashback; much of it is narrated by Mitchum, and its action has the force of a Freudian investigation into the past. Mitchum, an orphan adopted by Ma Callum (Judith Anderson), falls in love with his step-sister, Thorley (Teresa Wright). But Mitchum's attempts to find happiness are repeatedly thwarted by disruptive forces that have their roots in dimly remembered events in his own childhood: the sins of Mitchum's father and Thorley's mother (Anderson), whose illicit relationship is responsible for a feud between the Callums and the Rands, seem to plague Mitchum and Wright. Adam Callum (John Rodney), jealous of his sister's (Wright) love for outsider Mitchum, revives the feud that killed Mitchum's father and brothers years ago. Rodney ambushes Mitchum, who kills him in self-defense. Wright turns against Mitchum and then—with cold calculation—agrees to marry him: she plots to kill him on their wedding night to avenge her brother's death, but she unknowingly fires an empty gun at him, and this action purges her hatred.

The film concludes with a re-enactment of the traumatic event responsible for Mitchum's nightmares. Through a second shoot-out with his father's killer, Grant Callum (Dean Jagger), Mitchum rids himself of his obsession and gains the same psychological freedom Wright achieves when she forgets the past and embraces Mitchum after her unsuccessful attempt to kill him. Like a character in a Greek tragedy, Mitchum, initially nagged by doubts and fears, grows into an awareness of self and is liberated from the forces of the past which, like unseen furies, pursue him.

Mitchum's performance itself is a revelation. He makes convincing his successive transformations from an innocent, immature, identity-seeking youth into a rootless, unmotivated Spanish-American War veteran, a cynical gambler and the suitor of a girl who hates him, and finally, a mature man who freely accepts his past and its consequences. His eloquent performance gives the film's abstract psychological themes a flesh-and-blood reality, for it is through Mitchum that the film's ideas are expressed.

*PURSUED (1947). With Teresa Wright and John Rodney*

Back at RKO again, Mitchum appeared in *Crossfire* (1947), a taut, dark murder mystery. The murder victim, originally a homosexual in Richard Brooks' novel, is now a Jew, and the film becomes an indictment of anti-Semitism, following in the footsteps of Fox's *Gentleman's Agreement* (1947). The methods used by the police in capturing the racist killer, however, are a bit extreme. Police chief Robert Young lectures an ignorant soldier on the evils of prejudice. The soldier then plays *agent provocateur*, luring the suspected murderer back to the scene of the crime.

Mitchum plays Sergeant Keely, a demobilized veteran waiting out the remainder of his enlistment in Washington. His sole interest is in caring for his men, whose boredom, post-war despondency and undirected energy get them into trouble. When battle-fatigued Robert Ryan incriminates George Cooper, one of Mitchum's men, in the murder of Sam Levene, Mitchum conceals Cooper from the police and works outside the law to find the real murderer. Mitchum's dogged loyalty to his men, a carry-over from their wartime camaraderie, accentuates the difficulties involved in reintegrating G.I.s into post-war American society. Mitchum's plans backfire when a second murder occurs, and he reluctantly joins forces with Young.

CROSSFIRE (1947). With Robert Young

Mitchum, though lonely and at loose ends, holds himself together while the men around him fall apart. Mitchum's cool, controlled performance provides a counterpoint to the erratic, nervous, slightly manic behavior of Ryan, the shell-shocked murderer and anti-Semite. Young, on the other hand, seems casually unconcerned and even whimsical: as a man unfamiliar with the war veteran's psyche, he provides a contrast to both Mitchum and Ryan.

Jacques Tourneur's *Out of the Past* (1947) provided Mitchum with the best script and the first major role he had had since coming to RKO three years earlier. Written by Daniel Mainwaring under the pseudonym of Geoffrey Homes, the film's story immersed Mitchum in a dark, treacherous swirl of intrigue and passion. Mainwaring, who wrote pessimistic scripts for Phil Karlson's *The Phenix City Story* (1954) and Don Siegel's *Invasion of the Body Snatchers* (1957), conveys, though with considerably more wit, a similarly bleak vision of the world, a vision created in part by the hard-boiled detective genre of the period.

Mitchum plays Jeff Markham, a New York gumshoe. Unlike Bogart's bitter, sentimental but finally incorruptible detective in *The Maltese Falcon*, Mitchum, less particular about whom he works for or what he is asked to do, creates his own rules as he goes along. He shares Bogart's restlessness and romantic compassion, but he operates without ethics, remaining loyal only to himself. Hired by gangland kingpin Whit Sterling (Kirk Douglas) to retrieve an errant girlfriend (Jane Greer) who shot him before skipping the country, Mitchum follows her to Acapulco, where he falls in love with her at first sight as she walks out of the sunlight into a streetside cantina. Accused by Douglas of stealing $40,000, Greer protests her innocence to the cynical Mitchum. She concocts an obvious lie, then sweetly asks, "Don't you believe me?" He replies, "Baby, I don't care," and kisses her.

Subsequently abandoned by Greer after she sadistically and senselessly kills Mitchum's former partner, who has been trailing them for Douglas, Mitchum assumes the name of Jeff Bailey and settles down as a gas station operator in a small California town. He is discovered here at the beginning of the film by one of Douglas' men.

Douglas and Greer—she had pragmatically returned to Douglas for protection after killing Mitchum's partner—enlist Mitchum's aid on a job and attempt to frame him for murder. Mitchum sees through the frame-up, confronts Greer with it, and threatens her. But their battle for domination is one-sided: he lacks

*OUT OF THE PAST (1947). With Jane Greer and Kirk Douglas*

Greer's ruthlessness and her overpowering instinct for self-preservation. After all, she has had practice: she spends the greater part of the film betraying, framing and killing her lovers. When she realizes that Mitchum (on discovering she has killed Douglas) has informed the police, she shoots him in the groin, gets shot in turn by the police at a roadblock, and crashes their car into a roadside tree.

James Agee's criticism of Mitchum's performance singles out his "curious languor, which suggests Bing Crosby supersaturated with barbiturates" and his "sexual complacency." It is this very languor and complacency, however, that make Mitchum ideal for the part. His professional sloppiness—he uses the excuse of a closed Mexican telegraph office to sanction his failure to notify Douglas of

*OUT OF THE PAST (1947). With Jane Greer*

*RACHEL AND THE STRANGER (1948). With William Holden and Loretta Young*

Greer's whereabouts—involves him in a fatal, romantic complicity with Greer. He gets caught up in her sordid, psychotic life much as his naive girlfriend (Virginia Huston) becomes entangled in his.

Mitchum is a chameleon; his personality blends in with those of the people he is with, making him elusive. His identity as Jeff Bailey at the beginning of the film reflects the uncomplicated existence of a man who, in Mitchum's words, "used to be smart," who wants nothing more than to fish, pump a little gas now and then and forget the past.

When he is drawn back into the worldly milieu of New York gangsters and their molls, after a brief time of peace as Jeff Bailey, Mitchum finds himself turning

46

phrases and trading wisecracks with the rest of them, powerless to deny or repress a major part of his personality. At the end of the film, when Mitchum, unbeknownst to Greer, has decided to turn them both in, he celebrates by pouring out drinks and calmly reminiscing about their first meeting in Mexico. Greer sums up their misadventures, commenting, "We've had a lot of bad luck. . . . We deserve a break." Mitchum responds quickly, "We deserve each other," and dramatically throws his empty glass into the fireplace. His words and gesture signal a resigned realization that he cannot escape from his past or from his chaotic relationship with Greer.

Mitchum's languor, carelessness and romantic vulnerability transform *Out of the Past* into a romantic tragedy, whose moral scheme excludes any possibility of the hero's redemption. Tourneur's film acknowledges and reaffirms, through the Greer character, the power of evil in the world. This power lies chiefly in the debilitating fascination which evil holds for the film's characters, from the small-town girl who is attracted by Mitchum's mysterious past to Douglas and Mitchum themselves, who are fatally drawn to Greer. Mitchum's very human detective makes mistakes, giving him an unheroic mortality—his mistakes in character judgment literally lead to

his death—that sets him apart from most movie detectives. *Out of the Past* realizes as no other film does except *Angel Face*, the potential for self-destruction that lies within the Mitchum persona.

Schary exploited Mitchum's image of the romantic troubadour in *Rachel and the Stranger* (1948), a pre-Civil War frontier drama starring William Holden and Loretta Young. Mitchum plays a homeless, itinerant hunter whose rivalrous envy of Holden's home and family serves as a catalyst for the reconciliation of Holden and Young, his second wife. Mitchum is an old friend of the family, and there is a suggestion that his wanderlust—we first see him walking through the woods singing and playing his guitar—stems from his failure to win Susan, Holden's dead wife, in an earlier courtship.

After Mitchum's first visit, Holden buys and marries a bond woman (Young) to keep house and raise his boy. He treats her like a servant, comparing her unfavorably to his former wife. When Mitchum returns, the attentions he pays to Young make Holden jealous. Mitchum's backwoods charm, casual good looks and polite graciousness find a response in Young, who joins him in a lovely after-dinner duet. Their ease together contrasts with the nervous and starchy propriety which forces a repressive silence upon Holden's

RACHEL AND THE STRANGER (1948). With William Holden,
Gary Gray, and Loretta Young

relationship with Young.

When Mitchum, the perennial interloper, discovers that the marriage is loveless, he courts Rachel, openly declaring his intentions, and offers to buy her from Holden. When an Indian attack destroys the house that had been associated with Holden's dead wife, the barriers between Holden and Young are diminished, and they begin anew. Mitchum, typically unlucky in love, goes off with the men from a nearby fort in pursuit of the warring Shawnees.

Unconventional and disrespectful (especially of Holden's institutionalized conception of marriage), Mitchum's disruptive presence is clearly a liberating force in the film, although Young ultimately rejects his carefree existence in favor of a more stable life. Mitchum's role as the attractive but irresponsible

*BLOOD ON THE MOON (1948). With Barbara Bel Geddes*

hobo neatly counterbalances the film's more orderly civilizing impulses, further developing the anarchic aspects of his persona.

*Blood on the Moon* (1948), a classic *film noir* western, begins at night in the rain. Mitchum, an anonymous cowboy, unshaven and weary after a day's ride, slowly and methodically removes his boots and sets them to dry by a campfire. He prepares his meal with movements worn by lonely repetition. Out of the night a stampeding herd of cattle crashes through his camp, nearly trampling him to death, and a suspicious cattle rancher named Lufton (Tom Tully) threatens to shoot him unless he answers his questions. The atmosphere of fear and paranoia established in the film's opening sequence sets the tone for the remainder of this darkly lit and violent range-war western.

Apparently a "loose rider"

*THE RED PONY (1949). With Peter Miles*

named Jim Gary, unknown and un-
attached to the cattlemen or the
homesteaders, Mitchum is held and
questioned by Lufton, ambushed by
his daughter (Barbara Bel Geddes)
and treated inhospitably at Lufton's house after delivering an important note. Under suspicion of
being a range detective, he is questioned, tested and roughed up by
homesteaders who have been duped
by Reiling (Robert Preston) and his
gang of rustlers into opposing the

cattlemen. Mitchum is strangely at
home in this atmosphere of distrust and betrayal: although he is
defiantly angry at the Luftons for
his reception, he turns out to be ex-
actly what they imagine him to be:
one of Reiling's hired guns. But
even among Reiling's men, he remains aloof, unwilling to see himself as just another hired gun, and
when they try to kill him, he turns
against them.

Hawk-eyed and sneering,

Mitchum straddles the fence between the warring factions, committing himself to Lufton's side only after a brutal fight with Reiling. Playing the disillusioned, distrustful drifter persecuted by forces set in motion before his arrival and struggling to survive in a hostile setting, Mitchum turns in a complex performance that represents a complete transformation from his earlier, innocent incarnation as a two-dimensional Zane Grey hero in comparatively idyllic, small-scale westerns.

In *The Red Pony* (1949), Mitchum plays laconic hired hand Billy Buck, who helps a young boy (Peter Miles) care for and train a red pony. Based on a series of John Steinbeck stories, this film deals with the trials and hardships of ranch life. The action culminates in the illness and death of the boy's pony and the birth of a colt which Mitchum gives to the boy.

*Variety* singled out Mitchum's performance in this otherwise lackluster film: "As Billy Buck, the hired man, Robert Mitchum underscores a likeable role with a finely drawn portrayal of a grownup who understands both kids and horses. Mitchum once again demonstrates his flair for apt characterization without overplaying the faculty of getting at the emotional core of his audience."

In the fall of 1948, Mitchum, along with dancer Vicki Evans and real estate agent Robin Ford, was arrested in the rented Laurel Canyon home of actress Lila Leeds and charged with possession of marijuana. He was sentenced to sixty days in jail. During his sentence, Selznick sold his share of Mitchum's contract to Howard Hughes for $200,000. *Rachel and the Stranger* and *Blood on the Moon*, released after Mitchum's conviction, did well at the box office, indicating the public's continued support of the actor. Dore Schary left RKO to work for MGM at about this time, and Howard Hughes began to take a more personal interest in Mitchum's career.

At RKO, Mitchum never exercised much judgment in the selection of scripts. Towards the end of his contract there, he refused to do a number of films, but for the most part, he did whatever Hughes gave him. As he told one interviewer, "I've been making the same picture over and over again a hundred times. I didn't even look at the scripts, because I know, even if it was written by Baudelaire or Balzac, when I get to page twenty, a bunch of gorillas are going to jump out and start beating me up.

"Usually, you know, I make a film called *Pounded to Death by Gorillas*. They open up with a long shot of me standing and then a huge gorilla looms up behind and hits me on the top of the head. Boom, and I crumple. Boom. Boom. I keep falling down and getting up again. Then they cut to a little girl skipping through fields of daisies and finally she comes to this house and a voice says, 'Who's there?' As the writers haven't got that figured out yet, they cut back to me. Boom, boom, that gorilla is still knocking me down, and I'm still getting up again. Finally, the gorilla collapses on top of me, exhausted. Then the little girl comes in and says, 'He's around here someplace, I just know.' Finally, she peels away the gorilla and there lies our hero—me. So she hauls me to my feet, puts her arms around me, looks straight into

# THE HUGHES REGIME: POUNDED TO DEATH BY GORILLAS

the camera and says, 'I don't care what you think—*I like him*.' So you know he's got to be a hell of a man."*

Mitchum does indeed wrestle with a gorilla in the opening scene of Fox's *White Witch Doctor* (1953), and he wins. Though his other scripts from RKO and other studios may often have been ludicrous, they at least pitted him, for the most part, against somewhat less malodorous adversaries—like Jane Greer, Raymond Burr and Jack Palance.

According to director Don Siegel, the actor's next film, *The Big Steal* (1949), was an excuse to get Mitchum out of jail. Hughes used the project to pressure the court into releasing Mitchum, claiming that hundreds of other jobs were in jeopardy because of Mitchum's arrest and the film's delay. (Hughes had started the film while Mitchum was out on bail.) The plea was unsuccessful and the film was held up until Mitchum finished his sentence. "When Mitchum showed up for work, we

* Jerry Leblanc, *Newark Evening News*, October 12, 1968. Also quoted in Tomkies, *The Robert Mitchum Story*, p. 191.

*At the peak of his years with Howard Hughes*

*THE BIG STEAL (1949). With Jane Greer*

shot this picture in the heart of the marijuana district in Mexico, halfway between Vera Cruz and Mexico City. Mitchum showed up absolutely out cold, having drunk a bottle and a half of tequila with his probation officer, who if anything was drunker than Mitchum. It was quite a picture. . ."*

In the film, Mitchum plays an army finance officer who follows Patric Knowles, whom he suspects of robbing a government money shipment, to Mexico. William Bendix, a government agent, pursues Mitchum and Mexican police inspector Ramon Novarro tails them all. The film ends with an exciting chase sequence over rough Mexican countryside after which Mitchum, indirectly responsible for Knowles' payroll heist, clears himself with the American officials.

In *Holiday Affair* (1949), Mitchum plays an off-beat, anti-materialistic Santa Claus. Mitchum, again a drifter, meets widow Janet Leigh while working as a temporary clerk in a toy department during the Christmas rush. Leigh, a buyer for a rival store, dislikes Mitchum's unorthodox sales manner and gets him fired by the store manager. Despite this, his compulsive generosity remains intact, and he buys her son a coveted electric train with his last dollar. When he becomes inno-

* Interview with Don Siegel by Peter Bogdanovich, *Movie* #15, Spring, 1968.

cently involved in a park mugging, he is arrested and knowing nobody else in town, calls Leigh to bail him out.

Invited to Christmas dinner with Leigh and her fiancé, Wendell Corey, Mitchum rises after dinner and calmly proposes to Leigh. Not knowing whether Mitchum is insane, impossibly naive or merely tactless, Leigh refuses him, but while he waits for her to change her mind, she becomes attracted to him. After much soul-searching, Leigh decides she does love him and, breaking off with the more stable but less exciting Corey, leaves with Mitchum for California.

Brash, outspoken and uncompromising, Mitchum plays an absurdly unreal character, yet he gives this fairy-tale figure an honesty and integrity that make him almost convincing. Mitchum's charming, irresponsible vagabond is in the vanguard of the property-is-theft school of anarchism, despite the film's attempt to soften his radical impact with the trappings of domesticity (a wife, son and prospects of a steady job) at the end.

*Where Danger Lives* (1950), a vehicle designed to advance the career of Hughes' discovery, Faith Domergue, involves San Francisco intern Mitchum with the sexy but insane Domergue who murders her millionaire husband (Claude Rains), shifts the blame to

*HOLIDAY AFFAIR (1949). With Janet Leigh*

Mitchum and convinces him to run away. Again, Mitchum plays the familiar role of fall guy, a sucker for a sob story and a pretty face. Mitchum's romantic vulnerability receives further development in this John Farrow movie.

In *My Forbidden Past* (1951), Mitchum is little more than a male sex object for Ava Gardner. At the beginning of the film, cousin Melvyn Douglas' knowledge of the unsavory past of Gardner's mother prevents her from running off with Mitchum, a medical researcher. Stood up by Gardner, Mitchum sails alone from New Orleans for South America. He returns later with a wife (Janis Carter) and takes a research job at Tulane. Gardner, who has meanwhile inherited a fortune from a disreputable relative, is rebuffed in her attempts to lure Mitchum back, and she bribes her cousin to seduce Mitchum's wife, hoping to break up their marriage. During an argument with Douglas, the wife is killed, and the innocent

Mitchum is brought to trial for her murder. Though aware of Gardner's role in the affair, Mitchum stoically remains silent at the inquest. Gardner finally breaks down, confesses that her cousin is the murderer, and exposes both her disreputable lineage and her own complicity in the present scandal. Mitchum is freed. Gardner's action forges a tenuous reconciliation, and the movie ends with Mitchum comforting her.

Mitchum's unemotional inertia throughout the story, rather than lending strength to his character, merely serves to diminish his role in the film, turning him into a prize to be won or lost by Gardner. Mitchum is more passive than passionate in his relationship with Gardner, and the intensity which characterized his relationship with another *femme fatale*, Jane Greer, in *Out of the Past* is sadly lacking here.

Many of the films Mitchum made while Hughes was running RKO were tasteless, luridly sensational action and mystery pictures. The vulgar Hughes sex-and-violence formula, however, found a most fortuitous vehicle in *His Kind of Woman* (1951), a genre-mixing tongue-in-cheek *film noir* classic that can only be described as sub-

*WHERE DANGER LIVES (1950). With Faith Domergue*

*MY FORBIDDEN PAST (1951). With Ava Gardner*

limely ridiculous. Mitchum plays a small-time gambler named Milner whom deported gangster Nick Ferrar (Raymond Burr) hires, through agents, to wait for him in Mexico. Burr actually plans to assume Mitchum's identity in order to re-enter the States and to regain control of his underworld empire. On his way to a resort for a rendezvous with his mysterious contact, Mitchum meets Jane Russell, who is traveling to the same resort in the hope of snaring a movie actor (Vincent Price). The plot complications increase until the hysterically improbable finale: Price leads a band of Mexican police and hotel guests to rescue Mitchum, who has been beaten and is about to be injected with a mind-destroying drug.

During the film, a Price action picture is screened at the resort. One of the hotel's cynical guests, when asked by Price how he liked the film, says, "It has a message no pigeon would carry," a remarkably concise description of the typical Hughes product. In fact, the script repeatedly makes self-conscious references and in-jokes dealing with RKO, Hughes and Mitchum. At the beginning of the film, for example, there is even a reference to Mitchum's recent prison sentence. In an all-night diner, he mentions "doing thirty days" in Palm Springs. "For what?," he is asked, and Mitchum replies angrily, "For nothing."

The film is a strange combination of serious and comic elements. Paranoid and ridiculously unreal in its treatment of its characters' various commitments, it gives equal value to Mitchum's stoic suffering as he is sadistically tortured by Burr's men and to Price's hammy swashbuckling in his rescue attempt.

Mitchum, a victim of unseen forces, is practically driven to Mexico by Burr's syndicate. In addition to his inexplicable prison sentence, his wallet is stolen and he is beaten up, for no apparent reason, when he returns to his apartment. But he freely accepts the job. His curiosity, combined with his sense of adventure, prompt him to accept the strange offer of money and a trip to Mexico in exchange for as yet undisclosed services. Though curious, Mitchum is also withdrawn. Trying to find out why he has been sent there, he strikes up conversations with guests at the Morros Lodge, yet he answers rudely, almost hostilely, when questions are put to him by others. He has a characteristically unorthodox sense of right and wrong. He cheats at cards to help a young married couple get clear of their gambling debts; yet he not only refuses to honor his "agreement" with Burr but goes out of his way to turn him in.

Mitchum's teaming with Jane Russell presents two sides of the same coin: they wisecrack their way through love scenes, infusing them with just a suggestion of eroticism. No real love ever passes between them, yet there is a kind of off-beat sexual camaraderie, a cynical acceptance of one another as suitable objects of desire. His eyes give her the once-over when he first sees her in a border town cantina singing "Five Little Miles From San Berdoo." Initially a cynical gold-digger, a Russell role more fully realized in *Gentlemen Prefer Blondes* (1953) and *The Revolt of Mamie Stover* (1956), she immediately sizes Mitchum up for the irresponsible, itinerant gambler he is and brushes him off. But she realizes that he is as much her kind of man as she is his kind of woman. This fact becomes even more apparent in their next co-starring film, Josef von Sternberg's *Macao* (1952).

The interplay between Mitchum and Russell in *Macao*, as exotic as the film's Oriental locale, represents a transcendence of style over substance, a style that struggles out from under the weight of a mundane, mechanical plot. Mitchum, as petty smuggler and gambler Nick Cochran, and Russell, who plays

*HIS KIND OF WOMAN (1951). With Tim Holt and Jane Russell*

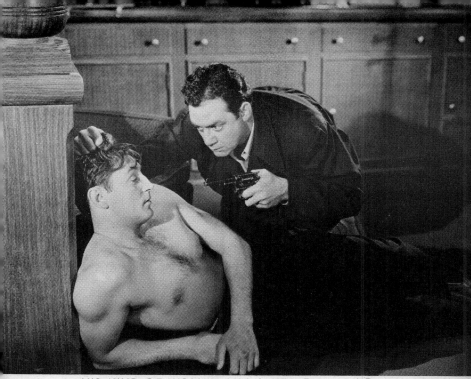

*HIS KIND OF WOMAN (1951). With Raymond Burr*

singer Julie Benson, become entangled in William Bendix's efforts to lure Brad Dexter, a mobster wanted for murder by the American police and the owner of Macao's "Quick Reward" casino, outside the three-mile limit so that he can be arrested.

Mitchum meets Russell on a boat when he is accidentally struck on the head by one of her shoes, intended for her lecherous male companion. Mitchum returns her shoe, knocks out her boisterous escort and rewards himself with a kiss. Later, on an upper deck, Bendix

gives Russell a pair of free-sample nylons. She throws her old stockings overboard and greedily puts on the new pair. Mitchum, watching on a lower deck, grabs one of the discarded stockings as it floats by, sniffs it sensually, and puts it in his breast pocket, discovering in the process that Russell lifted his wallet when he kissed her.

At their hotel, Mitchum enters Russell's room and rifles her purse while she takes a bath. They toss non sequiturs back and forth and trade insults, establishing a tempestuous rapport. Later in the

61

film, when Mitchum returns after being held captive by Gloria Grahame, Russell comes after him with an electric fan. He fends her off with a pillow and the room fills with fluttering feathers. Their relationship is more a fetishistic exchange and interplay of objects than of affection, yet they are more than sexual trophies to one another. Their initial wariness and shared distrust gradually mellow into a non-romantic, friendly acceptance of one another as individuals bound together by their common experience and shared loneliness. Both are worldly cynics, forced by their past or lifestyle to drift from port to port. In a way, they are perfect lovers. Russell's sullen feminine indolence complements Mitchum's casual masculine insolence. But beneath their animal sensuality lies a hollowness: they are merely exotic surfaces with no inner spirit.

Mitchum, cast as an unambitious, rootless adventurer, gives a characteristically elusive performance, underplaying his scenes with an intransigent indifference that, in the context of the other performances in the film, is remarkably expressive.

Sternberg's inspired direction of Mitchum and Russell's erotic encounters, however, only partially compensates for the film's unbearably trite plot. To further compli-

cate matters, Hughes began to meddle with the film and called in Nicholas Ray to reshoot about half of it. Sternberg subsequently disowned what proved to be his last Hollywood picture.

Between his two films with Russell, Mitchum starred in *The Racket* (1951), a remake of a Hughes-produced film released in 1928. Mitchum plays an incorruptible police captain opposite Robert Ryan, an Al Capone-type gangster. When Mitchum attempts to demolish Ryan's crime syndicate, Ryan tries to buy him off, then threatens him with a frame-up. He finally sends seductress Lizabeth Scott after him. Mitchum staunchly withstands Ryan's temptations and succeeds in destroying his organization. The movie was a standard melodrama, competently directed by John Cromwell.

Perhaps the worst Mitchum film under the Hughes regime is *One Minute to Zero* (1952), a nonsensical film about the Korean War. Mitchum plays Colonel Steve Janowsky, an American advisor to a group of South Korean troops at the outbreak of the war. Mitchum's militaristic behavior brings him into conflict with an unworldly, idealistic U.N. observer (Ann Blyth) whom he forcibly evacuates from Korea during an enemy attack. Later in the film, duty forces him to shell a column of refugees

*MACAO (1952). With Jane Russell*

*MACAO (1952). With Gloria Grahame*

heavily infiltrated by North Koreans. Blyth is shocked by his action and refuses to sign an affadavit of approval as U.N. representative, but she recants later when the facts of the shelling are explained to her.

The Blyth-Mitchum teaming has none of the Russell-Mitchum chemistry. Blyth replaced Claudette Colbert in the role when Colbert caught pneumonia midway through shooting on location in Colorado. Certainly Blyth looks out of place opposite Mitchum; she seems unreal, acting as if she had been parachuted into her part from the set of *Mildred Pierce* (1945). Mitchum sings to her over dinner in homespun Japanese and she sings back in operatic English, just one expression of the enormous disparity in style and personality between the two.

Director Tay Garnett typically fashions his films around such disparities, creating a range of moods and feelings that sets off the passion of his romantic leads, as in *One Way Passage* (1932). But *One Minute to Zero* has no emotional center to hold the peripheral pieces together.

The next two films Mitchum made at RKO, *The Lusty Men* (1952) and *Angel Face* (1952), are among his best. In *The Lusty Men*, Mitchum is cast as Jeff McCloud, an aging rodeo actor, a role that beautifully exploits the Mitchum persona. Lonely and homeless, Mitchum projects a feeling of vague, inarticulated discontent with

the life he leads. Yet his desire for something better is impeded by his own indecision and inertia.

Mitchum's rodeo life is rough and physically exacting, a contest of energy and will between him and the animals he rides. We first see him framed over the head of a Brahma bull which subsequently throws and gores him. Mitchum later talks of the "buzz" he gets from rodeoing, a temporary surge of vitality that comes only through riding. Separated from his profession, he is nothing: physically and emotionally worn, he limps painfully across the empty, litter-strewn

THE RACKET (1951). With Lizabeth Scott

*ONE MINUTE TO ZERO (1952). Colonel Steve with the men of his unit*

rodeo arena, forced by his injuries to quit.

Searching for something around which to build a new life, Mitchum goes back into the past. He returns to the ramshackle home he once escaped, "looking for something I thought I had lost." Mitchum crawls under the floor of the old McCloud place, now owned by a lonely, garrulous old man, and retrieves a childhood cache—two nickels and an old rodeo program. This is all he has after twenty years of rodeoing. He meets ranch hand Wes Merritt (Arthur Kennedy) and his wife Louise (Susan Hayward),

who want to buy his old place, dreaming of a home of their own. Kennedy recognizes the former rodeo star and gets him a job at his ranch. After Kennedy wins a few rodeo events himself, he and Mitchum form a partnership despite his wife's objections. Mitchum's search has been short and circular: he returns to rodeoing as Kennedy's manager.

Young, eager, and ambitious, Kennedy contrasts with Mitchum who is easy-going and unaggressive, but whose interest in Kennedy includes his wife. Hayward, the third corner of the triangle, understands Kennedy's dissatisfaction with his present life and shares his ambitious goals, but disapproves of the means he uses to reach them, fearing that he will become, like Mitchum, a rodeo bum. The Mitchum-Hayward relationship is built around shared cynicism, toughness, patient determination, and awareness of one another's goals. Hayward understands that she is Mitchum's chief interest, and he realizes that she tolerates him only because her husband needs him. They are worthy antagonists. Hayward tries to get Kennedy to quit rodeoing by making him jealous of Mitchum; Mitchum en-

courages Kennedy's rodeo career, hoping to lure Hayward away from him. The three-way relationship, built out of mutual and conflicting desires, becomes a microcosm of rodeo life in general: the eternal struggle to win an elusive prize.

After a brawl, Kennedy dissolves his partnership with Mitchum. In spite of Kennedy's refusal to give up rodeoing, Hayward decides to stay with him and not go off with Mitchum. Alone once again, Mitchum returns to the world that he abandoned and to which he really belongs. Existentially proving his independence, he responds to Kennedy's insults by

*THE LUSTY MEN (1952). With Susan Hayward*

ANGEL FACE (1952). With Jean Simmons

competing against him in the rodeo, even though he is out of shape and out of practice. His foot catches in a stirrup and he is dragged by a bronco, breaking his ribs and puncturing his lung. Mitchum achieves the heroism and significance in death that eluded him in life. His final heroic gesture is answered by Kennedy's equally courageous decision to return to ranching, the world to which he and Hayward belong, thus forging a permanent link of mutual indebtedness for what these three people helped one another achieve.

Director Nicholas Ray uses his characters as archetypes of a distinct class of people: rodeo people like Mitchum, Hayward and Kennedy have no homes or property; they are drifters. They live in cars and trailers, following the rodeo circuit from town to town. The men spend their free time gambling away their earnings in stables or drinking them up in bars. The women grow old before their time, praying that their husbands will not be gored, or crippled or killed by their profession. Although superficially glamorous, their life is brutal and unrewarding; it is a trap that must be escaped. Their only excitement is in a few minutes of competition; their only freedom is in death.

Based on real events made public during a celebrated contemporary trial, *Angel Face* is one of Otto Preminger's bleakest and most uncompromising films. Robert Mitchum plays Frank Jessup, an ambulance driver who is called to a Beverly Hills mansion on a late-night rescue mission. There he meets Diane Tremayne (Jean Simmons), whose stepmother, under mysterious circumstances, has nearly been asphyxiated by gas in her bedroom. On his way out of the house, Mitchum is strangely drawn to Simmons, whom he sees playing the piano in the living room. Their relationship is born out of a romantic curiosity in Mitchum that is as irresistible as it is irrational. Mitchum's openness to experience seems linked to an inner restlessness and discontent with what he already has, qualities which Ray and Preminger recognize in Mitchum and develop in their films with him.

In *Angel Face*, Preminger uses

ANGEL FACE (1952). With Jean Simmons

*WHITE WITCH DOCTOR (1953). With Susan Hayward and Walter Slezak*

these and other aspects of Mitchum's persona—his inertia and his lazy indecision—to trap him in a relationship that has no exit, and to involve him in a series of events that leads to his destruction. When Mitchum tells Simmons that her stepmother is alive, she becomes hysterical. He slaps her to calm her down, and she slaps him back. His relationship with Simmons begins and ends with violence, though her hysteria has turned to mad calculation by the film's conclusion. Simmons enters

Mitchum's life and, aided by his passivity, takes it over, beginning by ruining his relationship with his fiancée, Mary (Mona Freeman). Mitchum finds it impossible to resist Simmons' offer of a job as the family's chauffeur or to prevent his romantic involvement with her, even though he suspects her of trying to kill her stepmother.

Mitchum cannot say no. This trait of his screen persona, a fatal flaw in *Angel Face*, apparently has its roots in the real Mitchum. In an attempt to win early probation

70

after his marijuana conviction, Mitchum saw a psychoanalyst. According to Mitchum, the doctor "said I was suffering from a state of over-amiability, in which failure to please everyone created a condition of self-reproach. He told me I was going too far in seeking the good will of people and suggested that I risk their displeasure by learning to say 'no,' and following my own judgment."*

When Mitchum finally tries to leave, Simmons changes his mind. After she kills her stepmother and (accidentally) her father, she and Mitchum are arrested. Her attor-

ney, to win the jury's sympathy, asks Mitchum to marry her. He refuses, but then is forced by his own lawyer to change his mind. At the end of the film, Mitchum tries to flee her entrapment. He calls a cab, but Simmons convinces him to let her drive him to the bus station. As Mitchum complacently pours himself a farewell glass of champagne and barks angrily at her for causing him to spill it, she shifts her car into reverse and drives it backwards off a cliff, killing them both.

Simmons' passionate insanity is complicated by periods of lucidity in which she is guiltily aware of what she is doing or has done. Mitchum, though eminently sane,

* Interview with Dora Albert, *Silver Screen*, June, 1955.

*SECOND CHANCE (1953). With Jack Palance and Linda Darnell in the cable car climax*

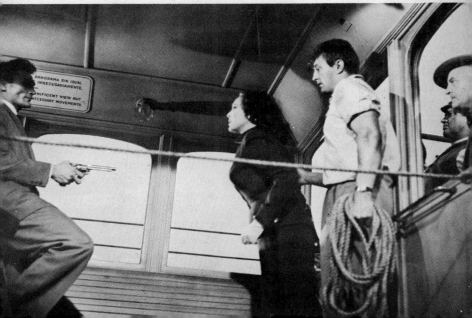

*SHE COULDN'T SAY NO (1954). With Jean Simmons*

has no corresponding moments of perspective from which he can view his actions. His scenes with Simmons show he is only dimly aware of what is going on within her and within himself. Caught up in Simmons' dreamlike perceptions of the world, he realizes what has happened only after it is too late to prevent it. He has no control over his destiny. In *Angel Face*, Mitchum lives for and by the moment, surrendering himself to the stronger personalities around him.

In *White Witch Doctor* (1953), Mitchum, on loan to 20th Century-Fox, was again teamed with Susan Hayward in a Technicolor jungle adventure. The film begins with the escape of a caged gorilla. Mitchum, a professional trapper, prevents the terrified natives from killing the animal and wrestles it to the ground. Hayward, a recently arrived missionary, fearing the gorilla might have killed someone before Mitchum subdued it, criticizes him for taking chances. Mitchum cynically replies that "a live gorilla is worth five hundred francs." Hayward self-righteously asks, "How much is a human life worth?" and an exhausted Mitchum quips, "I don't know. I just trap animals. I leave humans to the missionaries."

"White Witch Doctor" Hayward and Great White Hunter Mitchum carry their missionary-mercenary antagonism with them into the jungle, where their toughness towards one another softens into love. Though Mitchum, playing a cynical, Bible-quoting, pipe-smoking man of action, gives the film character, *White Witch Doctor* is a collection of jungle film clichés, adequately directed by Henry Hathaway.

Back at RKO, Mitchum starred in *Second Chance* (1953) a beautifully photographed romantic adventure story, filmed in Mexico in the then-popular 3-D process. As boxer Russ Lambert, Mitchum is a self-willed expatriate who has killed another fighter in the States; now he fights second-raters in Mexico, winning on decisions because he is afraid to throw his right. Mitchum plays the fighter as a broken-down celebrity, friendly with bartenders and full of come-on lines for the girls. Like Mitchum, Linda Darnell is also on the run from her past, hiding out in Mexico from a gangster who fears her testimony. Pursued by the gangster's hit man (Jack Palance), Darnell uses Mitchum, without his knowledge, to elude Palance. The story's climax involves Mitchum and Palance's life-and-death struggle in an aerial car with a snapped cable.

Mitchum and Darnell make a good combination. Darnell's worldliness, moral ambivalence, casual distrust of men, and proud self-confidence evoke a protective tenderness in Mitchum, who shares and admires many of her characteristics.

Mitchum's last film for RKO was *She Couldn't Say No* (1954), a comedy teaming him again with Jean Simmons. In the film, Simmons inherits a fortune and returns to the small town of Progress, Arkansas, intent on rewarding its citizens for having once saved her life. Years before the film begins, they took up a collection and sent her, as a two-year-old, to a clinic in St. Louis for a critical operation. Her philanthropy backfires, corrupting the once innocent town. Mitchum plays an unambitious young country doctor who, initially suspecting that the eccentric Simmons is insane, observes her and later tries to prevent her from spoiling the simple life of the town's inhabitants. The patient Mitchum spends half his time fishing for an elusive catfish with a local youngster, and the other half sorting out the problems caused by Simmons' charity. He barely saves the town drunk (Arthur Hunnicutt) from acute alcohol poisoning and grudgingly serves as veterinarian when the local vet, helped by Simmons, leaves for California. Simmons eventually makes a public apology and Mitchum, taking her in his charge, proposes to her.

Mitchum, near the end of his contract, began to feud with Hughes over the parts he was given. He made a special point of not flying with TWA (Hughes' airline) whenever he went anywhere, and actively proclaimed his defiance of Hughes by refusing to star in *Cattle Queen of Montana* (1954) or in *The French Line* (1954), a 3-D vehicle for Jane Russell. Hughes suspended him, and Mitchum worked out the remaining films in his RKO contract on loan-out to other studios. Mitchum left RKO just before its demise; Hughes sold the studio in July of 1955, and it went out of business soon afterwards.

Free of Howard Hughes and RKO, Mitchum now began to take control over the parts he played and deliberately set about to broaden his image. He immediately took parts as the irredeemably nasty elder brother in *Track of the Cat* (1954), the idealistic doctor in *Not as a Stranger* (1955) and the sadistic preacher in *The Night of the Hunter* (1955), actively testing the moral limits of his screen persona. Though the films themselves were not always successful, Mitchum demonstrated a versatility and professionalism that had been ignored by RKO.

Mitchum's best performance of this period, though his role was more conventional, was in Otto Preminger's *River of No Return* (1954), a CinemaScope western for Fox. Pursued by Indians and in pursuit of a gambler (Rory Calhoun) who has stolen his horse and gun, Mitchum pilots a raft, together with his son (Tommy Rettig) and the gambler's girl (Marilyn Monroe), downriver through a treacherous series of rapids.

The Mitchum characters in his two Preminger films are radically different: Mitchum here has few of the negative characteristics he had in *Angel Face*. No longer a loser, he is cast as Matt Calder, a frontier farmer and responsible father. He has a strong sense of self; he is rugged and self-sufficient and

## SYMPATHY FOR THE DEVIL

knows what he wants; he plays a stronger, more mature, less vulnerable character than he had ever played before.

Matt lives according to a primitive frontier morality. Though he once shot a man in the back and was imprisoned for it, his action was honorable and necessary: he did it to save the life of a friend. His past is less of a problem to him than it is to his son, who cannot understand or approve his father's action until he himself is faced with a similar predicament. At the same time, Mitchum disapproves of Monroe, justly questioning her loyalty to the shiftless Calhoun, and he treats her like a common dance-hall girl.

Mitchum's physical strength (in a pre-credit sequence he fells an enormous tree) and his simple rustic morality (shown initially in his disdain for the behavior of the people in the gold boom town) are the cornerstones on which half of the film is built. The other half stands on the very different moral strengths and weaknesses embodied in Monroe.

Mitchum's single-mindedness of purpose becomes visually evident when he searches for his boy in the gold town. He enters a saloon in

*RIVER OF NO RETURN (1954). With Marilyn Monroe*

which Monroe is singing and circles the bar, ignoring her and the drunks around her. Mitchum's limited concerns narrow his perspective and cause him to appear withdrawn: he cares only about finding his boy and returning to his farm. Monroe sings "One Silver Dollar" and "I'm Gonna File My Claim," songs about selfish golddiggers like herself. But as an entertainer, she is outgoing and she relates to her audience, providing a contrast to Mitchum in his preoccupation with his own affairs. Yet her concerns and her world are just as limited as Mitchum's, if not more so. This scene epitomizes their relationship: they share the same physical space, but ignorant of one another's feelings and desires, they exist in two different worlds.

Mitchum and Jane Russell may be two sides of the same coin, but Mitchum and Monroe are diametric opposites. Mitchum is earthy and physical; Monroe is artificial and superficial. Mitchum is real; his presence is concrete. Monroe, as Howard Hawks realized in *Gentlemen Prefer Blondes*, is essentially phony and, as he points out, "a complete fantasy." Mitchum has a strength that is rooted in his worldliness. Monroe has a naive vulnerability, relying as she does on illusions.

In both *Angel Face* and *River of No Return*, Preminger casts Mitchum with women who are antithetical to him. Mitchum's middle-class ambulance driver and chauffeur in *Angel Face* gets involved with a high-class society girl.

His vernacular American speech contrasts with her more cultivated English accent and his hard-headed sanity clashes with her passionate insanity. Mitchum and Simmons, like Mitchum and Monroe in the later film, inhabit two different worlds, worlds that have only a few crucial points in common. The bits and pieces of their shared experiences in *Angel Face* work themselves out in a chaotic and confused way to a tragic conclusion. In the more open-ended *River of No Return*, Mitchum and Monroe take paths that are different but not hostile or counter-productive: they lead in roughly the same direction and result in an affirmative reconciliation between the two. Mitchum and Monroe come to share, as a result of their moral and emotional odyssey on the river, more and more points in common. They change gradually over a period of time until their distant tolerance of one another grows into mutual respect.

The stagy and symbolic script of *Track of the Cat* (1954), though based on a novel by Walter Van Tilburg Clark, could have been written by Eugene O'Neill. The film deals with the melodramatic events in the life of an isolated Montana family. The father (Philip Tonge) drinks and spouts Polonian sentiments. The spinster daughter (Teresa Wright) becomes, through the course of the film, increasingly unstable. The youngest son (Tab Hunter) is weak and indecisive, afraid to ask his girl (Diana Lynn) to marry him and reluctant to set out on his own. The family is run by a cold and spiteful mother (Beulah Bondi) who falls apart when her eldest son dies. Another son, the mean-spirited, vulgar Curt (Mitchum), runs the ranch and tyrannizes his brothers. In this allegorical tale, the family and the ranch are terrorized by an unseen panther called "the black painter," which, according to director William Wellman, is a "symbol of evil."

The despicable Mitchum, bearded and with a wicked glint in his eyes, growls through his role, sneering at the weaknesses of those around him. He ridicules Hunter in front of Lynn, his fiancée, saying he has "the spirit of a gelding," and then makes a play for Lynn himself, bragging that he will bring back a big panther skin for her bed. Though the family is a collection of loners and odd-balls, Mitchum's masculine self-confidence, aggressiveness, and unrepressed sexual drive single him out for attention. He gives his two-dimensional, evil character positive qualities as well: honesty, energy and ambition. Though he keeps his family under his thumb, it is the force of his will that holds them together, made clear by their disintegration at his death.

*RIVER OF NO RETURN* (1954). With Marilyn Monroe

*TRACK OF THE CAT (1954). As Curt*

After the panther kills his older brother (William Hopper), Mitchum tracks it into the hills. Exhausted and short of food, he gradually cracks up. He holds his head in his hands, talks to himself and to his dead brother, and even reads his brother's volume of Keats. He is killed by the panther, and Hunter, who is now forced to act on his own, proves himself by shooting the cat.

Mitchum, who usually underplays his parts, pulls out all the stops in this role as the raunchy, abrasive, lecherous, self-important Curt. His death leaves a gaping hole in the film that the drab Tab Hunter never quite fills. The film itself is a glum and turgid effort that comes to life only sporadically.

After *Track of the Cat*, Wellman signed Mitchum for a role in the Batjac production of *Blood Alley* (1955). Mitchum was fired for participating in a series of pranks that Wellman considered detrimental to the making of the film. He was replaced by John Wayne.

In *Not as a Stranger* (1955), producer Stanley Kramer, in his first film as a director, cast Mitchum against type as an idealistic young doctor. Mitchum plays Lucas Marsh, an impoverished, starving medical student whose dissolute father drinks up his tuition money,

*NOT AS A STRANGER (1955). With Gloria Grahame*

*THE NIGHT OF THE HUNTER (1955). As Preacher Harry Powell*

forcing him to skip meals and scrounge for money. Ruthless in his determination to become a doctor, he marries a Swedish nurse (Olivia de Havilland) for her money and, with her help, finishes medical school.

Joyless, humorless and loveless, he becomes a martyr to his ideals, sacrificing his personal humanity in order to serve humanity in general. Surrounded by more mercenary students like Frank Sinatra and Lee Marvin, Mitchum smugly condemns their less idealistic motives and criticizes their lack of medical expertise. His own perfectionism leaves no room for concern with the feelings of other, less perfect people.

Kramer seems much more sym-

pathetic to Mitchum's heartless super-doctor than he should be, but he nonetheless uses him to take a few swipes at the hypocrisy of the medical profession. When compared to the Lloyd C. Douglas-Frank Borzage treatments of similar characters and concerns in *Green Light* (1937) and *Disputed Passage* (1939), *Not as a Stranger* reveals Kramer's hollow concern for humanity and inflated interest in abstract issues.

Kramer's overstatement and his use of broad stylistic touches turn his characters into caricatures; they become flat, cardboard cut-outs that are maneuvered through the melodramatic machinery of Morton Thompson's stormy narrative. Mitchum's performance, however, is admirably suited to the film's style: his empty expression provides Kramer with the blank surface he needs to write out his messages.

*The Night of the Hunter* was Charles Laughton's first (and only) picture as director and James Agee's last screenplay. Laughton and Agee prepared the script while screening D. W. Griffith films, and the Griffith influence is considerable, extending not only to the casting of Lillian Gish (and the character she plays) but to the construction of the film's allegorical plot. The film *looks* like an amalgam of Griffith's *The Avenging Conscience* (1914), *Way Down East* (1920) and *Dream Street* (1921), a look that can best be described as "rustic expressionism."

The story deals with a backwoods "preacher" (Mitchum) who marries women for their money, then murders them. He marries drab religious fanatic Willa Harper (Shelley Winters) for the money her dead husband stole and hid. After he kills her, her two young children escape with the money, and he pursues them across the Ohio River Valley countryside. The terrified children are taken in by the gentle but resilient Mrs. Cooper (Lillian Gish), and Mitchum is caught and arrested.

The film begins with passages from the Bible, read by Gish, which identify the film as a religious fable.

The characters in this fable are suitably flat and symbolic; like figures in a children's fairy tale, they lack the psychological depth of conventional movie characters. They are understood not as flesh-and-blood people, but rather as the personifications of the larger moral forces at work in the film. Mitchum, as Preacher, plays a gothic villain. He represents a distorted conception of religion: vengeful and sexually repressive, he kills women he considers to be adulterous, lustful or evil.

During the film, he preaches a sermon about the eternal struggle between love and hate. The words "love" and "hate," tattooed on his right and left hands, reflect his simplistic, external approach to morality; it is a kind of wrestling match between two opposing forces, a contest the film realizes in its final confrontation between Gish and Mitchum.

In contrast to Mitchum's religious hypocrisy stands Gish's sincere and practical application of religious precepts. She takes in homeless and unwanted children and loves and protects them. She keeps a night-long vigil, holding a rifle on her lap, when Mitchum comes after the Harper children.

The differences between Mitchum and Gish emerge clearly during this vigil, as Gish joins Mitchum in singing a religious hymn ("The Everlasting Arms"),

*THE NIGHT OF THE HUNTER (1955). With Shelley Winters*

*THE NIGHT OF THE HUNTER (1955). With Billy Chapin and Sally Jane Bruce*

crystallizing their contrasting attitudes toward religion. Mitchum's rendition of the song is chilling and threatening, recalling the song's earlier associations with his demonic pursuit of the children. Gish sings the hymn sweetly and innocently, restoring its force as a song of faith and comfort.

Mitchum, though unconvincing in his first scene when he talks to God, ably portrays the half conman, half psychotic Preacher. He crooks his head and uplifts his hands in a way that suggests Satanic possession, and his condescension when speaking to Winters or her children is particularly terrifying. His feigned tears over Winters' supposed departure are appropriately evasive and unemotional. The last half of the film transforms him into a brutal animal. Hands outstretched, he reaches for the children (like a Griffith villain out of *Orphans of the Storm*), struggling up basement stairways and lunging through dense thickets.

Agee, who never understood Mitchum's romantic potential,

leaves unrealized Mitchum's scenes with Winters. He magnifies Mitchum's oiliness and his brutal unconcern for her feelings, but ignores the actor's talent for ingratiating, insidious tenderness. As a result, Mitchum merely victimizes, and Winters calmly accepts her fate.

Laughton's ambitiously headstrong direction of the film finally loses touch with Mitchum's primal earthiness, and the symbolic aspects of the film come to dominate the more immediate reality of character. Mitchum's initially powerful presence becomes more and more abstract and shadowy, giving up ground to the fragile-looking but tough Lillian Gish, who steals the picture from him.

On March 8, 1955, Mitchum, following precedents set by other top male stars, formed his own company, DRM Productions (combining his wife's and his own initials), and made a five-picture deal with United Artists for release of his films. Mitchum's personality had never been suited to studio supervision, contracts and regulations; now he was his own boss. Mitchum's choice of projects for himself was surprisingly commercial and unimaginative at first (*Man With The Gun*, 1955; *Foreign Intrigue*, 1956; and *Bandido*, 1956). But he soon began to make more personal films: *Thunder Road* (1958), *The Wonderful Country* (1959) and *The Night Fighters* (1960). Mitchum, clearly the creative force behind these last three projects, emerged, alongside John Wayne, as one of the most original of the actor-producers of the fifties.

In *Man With The Gun* (1955), an adult western produced by Samuel Goldwyn, Jr. and directed by Richard Wilson, Mitchum plays a Hamlet-like gunfighter named Clint Tollinger. Always dressed in grey, he somberly wanders the west, neither good-guy nor bad-guy, taming towns and restoring law and order. Melancholy and bitter, he remains an outsider, disliked equally by the honest and the dishonest citizens of the town. "There are no rules in my end of the business but one," he tells the friendly town blacksmith. "Don't stay in one town for too long!"

Mitchum's rootlessness is once again linked to a mysterious past—a father who was killed by land-grabbers, a former wife (Jan Sterling) who deserted him because of his violent profession and who is now madam of the town's brothel, and a missing daughter. Mitchum is a cold-blooded, experienced professional; his town-taming is part gun-play and part strategy. Like John Wayne in *Rio Bravo* (1959), he engages in a battle of wits with his unseen opponent,

MAN WITH THE GUN (1955). With Jan Sterling

finally outfoxing him and luring him into town.

Mitchum's icy self-control breaks down only once. When he learns from his wife that their daughter is dead, he goes berserk, demolishes the local saloon, forces its owner into a fight, then burns it down, almost setting fire to the rest of the town as well. Mitchum's rediscovery of feelings he thought he had lost reunites him with his wife (who later helps to save his life). Rejecting lives built on the corruption of others, they make a fresh start after Mitchum finishes cleaning up the town.

*Foreign Intrigue* (1956) written and directed by television *wünderkind* Sheldon Reynolds, should have been a good picture. It was based on Reynolds' popular television series. It had colorful European locations and also an excellent screenplay about the investigations of a press agent (Mitchum) into the mysterious past of his dead employer, Victor Dannemor. Welles had done something similar the year before in *Mr. Arkadin* (1955)—and in *Citizen Kane*, for that matter—but Reynolds adds a new twist: Dannemor knew that four important men had contracted with Hitler to betray their countries, but their countries (Switzerland, England, Sweden and the U.S.A.) had never been invaded. It turns out that Dannemor himself was one of the four men and was blackmailing the three others when he was murdered.

Despite its credentials, the final film is a complete failure, largely owing to Reynolds' poor direction. It is full of interminable shots of Mitchum in his trench coat, walking the dark, deserted streets of Vienna or trudging along the bright, colorful streets of Stockholm. Mitchum is merely a walking trench coat—there is no character inside it. Mitchum's motivation is unclear: we never understand why he starts his investigation, whether out of curiosity or greed (hoping to do some blackmailing himself). He is cast as a romantic lead, but his love scenes with Ingrid Thulin are unbelievably mechanical and businesslike. He is more convincing as the cynical lover of Dannemor's treacherous widow (Genevieve Page).

In *Bandido* (1956), a film coproduced by Mitchum, he plays a gun-runner during the Mexican rebellion of 1916. He checks into a hotel in a war-torn town and cynically watches the fighting in the streets below his balcony window, occasionally tossing a grenade to keep things moving. The soldier-of-fortune role is an ideal part for Mitchum, meshing beautifully with his amoral image.

After *Bandido*, Mitchum signed a three-year contract with 20th Century-Fox. He was cast in *Boy on a Dolphin* (1957), opposite Mar-

*FOREIGN INTRIGUE (1956). As Bishop, under the gun*

lon Brando but when Brando rejected the part, the film was delayed and Mitchum was put to work on John Huston's *Heaven Knows, Mr. Allison* (1957), in which he played one of his best-remembered roles. In this film, marine corporal Mitchum is stranded during World War II on a deserted island in the South Pacific with a nun, Sister Angela (Deborah Kerr). Their island is invaded by the Japanese twice, but is finally taken by the Americans.

Mitchum's character as the tough, disciplined marine is established at the beginning of the film when he "takes" the deserted island, swimming ashore, crawling through underbrush and checking abandoned buildings for traces of the enemy. Yet his training goes back much further than jungle survival tactics to an awkward set of manners, acquired in an orphanage: exhausted, he politely asks Kerr if it is all right for him to pass out in her church. Throughout the film, they address one another as "ma'am" and "Mr. Allison", and John Lee Mahin's screenplay gives the unpolished soldier deliberately strained and formal dialogue: when Kerr leaves their cave to look for

Mitchum who is missing, he returns and scolds, "I'm very put out with you, ma'am."

Initially, their formality with one another is superficial. He respects her as a nun, and she, half in wonder at and half in fear of his marine mentality, adds to the respectful distance between them. The film, however, breaks down the charming formality of their relationship. Mitchum, drunk on Japanese sake, loses a bit of his army indoctrination and tells her they've been by-passed by the American forces and might spend years alone together on the island. Singing "Don't sit under the apple tree with anyone else but me" to her, he starts talking about Adam and Eve, and she, foolishly fearing him, runs out into a rainstorm subsequently developing a fever through which he tenderly nurses her.

Like Huston characters in other films, they gain from their experiences a respect and admiration for each other's uniqueness. He respects her decision to remain a nun, and she understands his determination to rejoin the marines (which he does by disabling Japanese shore defenses). Earlier in the film, Mitchum, dimly aware of their deeper kinship, tells Kerr, "I've got the corps like you've got the church. . . . You've got your cross. I've got my globe and anchor."

Mitchum and Kerr play beautifully opposite one another. Mitchum's unshaven, lower class, coarse, prejudiced marine becomes a child in her presence, giving her flowers and carving her a crude wooden comb. Clearly, Mitchum is as baffled by her as she is by him.

Mitchum has a tremendously physical presence in this film; he visibly takes a good deal of punish-

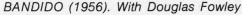

*BANDIDO (1956). With Douglas Fowley*

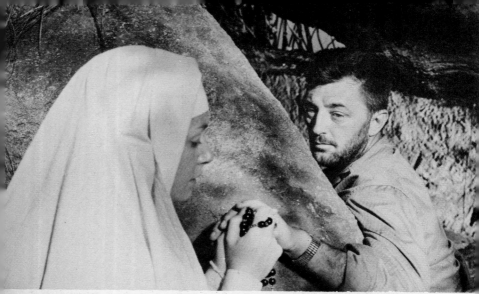

*HEAVEN KNOWS, MR. ALLISON (1957). With Deborah Kerr*

ment when he is catching turtles or eluding Japanese patrol boats in the surf, and his physicality becomes a crucial part of the earthy immediacy of his performance. Kerr is less at ease physically, and her awkwardness extends to her behavior with Mitchum. Her unfamiliarity with worldly experience contrasts with his worldliness; their combination brings out the innocence of each.

Mitchum plays Allison without condescension or unnecessary buffoonery. He realizes the maximum out of the situation's comic potential without forcing or belaboring his understated acting style. Mitchum and Kerr carry the film without faltering—something which few two-person casts have ever done—and establish a non-

romantic vitality and honesty in their male-female relationship that is uncommon in commercial films.

Columbia's *Fire Down Below* (1957) marked Rita Hayworth's return to the screen after her divorce from singer Dick Haymes. Appropriately enough, Robert Mitchum and Jack Lemmon fight over her, picking up where the action of her last picture, *Miss Sadie Thompson* (1954), left off. Caribbean smugglers Felix (Mitchum) and Tony (Lemmon) agree to transport war refugee Irena (Hayworth) to another island, sneaking her past immigration officials.

Mitchum, in a part that exploits the purely physical aspects of his sexual appeal, is brutally masculine: deep-chested and trim waisted, he wears tight-fitting striped polo shirts, drinks brandy, and smokes big cigars. No gentleman, he usually wears a straw hat indoors, and when he feels good he slaps his muscle-hard stomach. At first he is reluctant to take the Hayworth job, distrusting her and the set-up. When he goes to meet her in a bar, he moves across the room with the fluid grace of an animal stalking its prey. At her table, he gives her a long, cool, knowing stare that is both insulting and interested. After he leaves, Hayworth, less insulted than amazed, comments on the sexual insolence of his presence: "Sometimes you wonder what God had in mind when he invented the male sex!"

Mitchum immediately sizes Hayworth up, with "her sad, pitiful eyes and sweet, poisonous mouth," as a tramp. When Lemmon starts looking boyishly and longingly at her, he tries to separate them. Mitchum accuses Hayworth of being an ex-Nazi. Lemmon, accusing Mitchum in turn of "trying to be chosen for the brute-of-the-month club," gallantly comes to Hayworth's defense, and the two friends almost kill one another in a violent fist fight.

Mitchum and Hayworth respond to one another at a sensual, animal level. Excited by her erotic beauty in a Mardi Gras dance, Mitchum later bursts into her cabin and tries but fails to rape her. Lemmon's interest in Hayworth, on the other hand, is more innocent and romantic. Adolescently infatuated, he

*HEAVEN KNOWS, MR. ALLISON (1957). With Deborah Kerr*

*FIRE DOWN BELOW* (1957). As Felix

asks her to marry him. Trying to discourage Lemmon, the only man who has ever been nice to her, Hayworth tells him that she is what Mitchum thinks she is, a woman who has been "passed from hand to hand." Unconvinced, Lemmon naively repeats his offer of marriage.

In order to raise some money for a trip to the States, Lemmon plans one more smuggling venture. Mitchum, angry at his friend for falling for a tramp; and jealous as well, refuses to go along; he is too busy getting drunk on Jamaican rum. Mitchum subsequently betrays Lemmon, turning him in to the customs officials. While Lemmon is away, the unfaithful Hayworth and an unequally disloyal Mitchum, unable to resist one another, become lovers. Mitchum later explains to Lemmon: "She's the only thing I ever really wanted."

The film makes full use of the differences in type between Mitchum and Lemmon. Mitchum, lower-class, crude, violent and vulgar, is the scum of the earth. Like Hayworth, he leaves a trail of ruin wherever he goes. Cynical and treacherous, he lets his desires govern his behavior. He does what he must to get what he wants, and this ruthlessness he shares with Hayworth. Lemmon, less experienced and more civilized than Mitchum, is archetypally middle-class. His actions, unlike Mitchum's, are governed by conventional morality, as are his goals: he offers Hayworth marriage, a home and an opportunity to make something out of her life. Lemmon believes in romantic redemption. Mitchum believes in and offers to Hayworth nothing but himself.

Hayworth's choice, like that of Sadie Thompson, is less intellectual than emotional. A creature of instinct and passion, she chooses Mitchum. And she seems to enjoy waiting for him during cock fights, sitting with him in bars and drifting with him from port to port. *Fire Down Below* actually makes Mitchum's immorality attractive; it becomes a positive feature, winning him Rita Hayworth.

To complete his Fox contract, Mitchum made two fine films for producer-director Dick Powell, *The Enemy Below* (1957) and *The Hunters* (1958), both tautly written by Wendell Mayes. In *The Enemy Below*, Mitchum plays the hard, crafty captain of an American destroyer stalking an elusive German submarine in the South Atlantic during World War II. Mitchum is tough and experienced: he spent twenty-five days on a life-raft after his last ship was torpedoed. Even though his wife was killed at sea on a freighter that was also torpedoed, Mitchum is professional about his job, showing no traces of personal animosity toward his Ger-

*FIRE DOWN BELOW (1957). With Jack Lemmon and Rita Hayworth*

man counterpart.

The real star of the film is not Mitchum but the carefully plotted screenplay which pits Mitchum against U-boat captain Curt Jurgens in a tense battle of tactics, strategy and wits. Mitchum enjoys his role as hunter, tracking and anticipating Jurgens' movements, and he takes a special delight in discovering that there is a mind of equal intelligence at the other end of his sonar beam.

The film ends with Mitchum and Jurgens destroying each other's boats. Mitchum rescues Jurgens (whose loyalty to his wounded mate forces him to stay on the doomed sub), and both are picked up by an American ship. Their exchange of looks at the end reveals a professional respect. Their isolation from one another as enemies is breached momentarily by this mutual respect and by the common isolation of captains burdened with the lonely responsibility of command.

Mitchum was originally considered for the part of Dean Hess in Douglas Sirk's *Battle Hymn* (1956), but Hess rejected Mitchum, explaining, "I couldn't allow an actor who had been jailed for taking drugs to play me on the screen." Hess approved Rock Hudson, and Mitchum instead made *The Hunters*, a film that is in some ways similar to *Battle Hymn*. He is cast as Major Cleve Saville, a World War II and Korean War flying ace.

An old war buddy describes him to the young recruits as "a big hunter, the ice man," complimenting Mitchum's professional approach to war. As in *The Enemy Below*, he is crafty: he outwits the unit's best pilot in simulated combat arranged as a test.

A career officer, Mitchum is coolly professional about his participation in the war. Unlike some of his men, he is able to leave his personal problems on the ground when he goes on a mission. Abbott (Richard Egan), a weak and insecure pilot, admires Mitchum and comments, "He's like death—no feelings, no nerves, no fears . . ."

Mitchum and the other men are cynical and unpatriotic. Egan's neglected wife (May Britt), with whom Mitchum falls in love, asks him, "Do you like the war?" Mitchum replies, "It's the only war I've got." Mitchum's old World War II buddy complains that "you can't *feel* this war." Robert Wagner, an arrogant young pilot whose selfishness results in another pilot's death, wants only to shoot down planes and balks at Mitchum's orders. All of the men, for various reasons, suffer from a paralysis of the emotions.

*The Hunters* exploits Mitchum's image as a man without emotions, but in the end it surprises us by finally showing that he does have feelings. Egan is shot down behind enemy lines. Mitchum could easily leave the wounded Egan there to be shot by approaching Korean soldiers, but his own personal code, his sense of fairness and the honesty and openness of his relationship with both Britt and Egan prompt him to risk his own life to attempt a rescue. Mitchum's sentimental

*THE ENEMY BELOW (1957). With David Hedison*

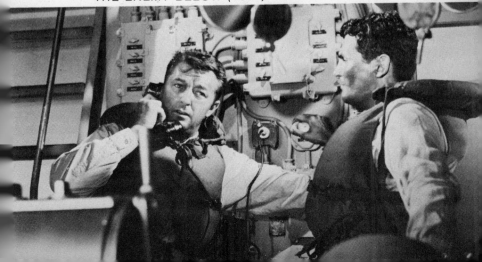

*THE HUNTERS (1958). With May Britt*

gesture makes him human and adds a note of personal warmth to his cold professionalism.

Britt is unable to leave Egan, who now needs her, and Mitchum returns to his lonely career. As in *Heaven Knows, Mr. Allison*, both the lovers have prior commitments and respect each other's decisions to abide by them. When they part, Mitchum suppresses his feelings for her; he calls her "Mrs. Abbott" instead of his customary "Christina." As she leaves, she turns to wave good-bye. Mitchum, studying a formation of jets in the sky above, doesn't see her.

*Thunder Road* (1958) is probably Robert Mitchum's most personal work. Mitchum produced it, starred in it, wrote the original story on which it is based, and even composed its title song (sung by Keely Smith). It is a film that, more than any other, reveals Mitchum's awareness of his own screen personality.

He casts himself as Luke Doolan, a moonshine runner who drives his father's illegal alcohol out of the hills past the government agents to distribution points in the city. Characteristically, Mitchum is a loner; he boasts, "I don't buddy up with one livin' soul." The illegality of his profession makes him an outlaw, and his experiences in the Korean War alienate him from the other less worldly moonshiners in his valley. Mitchum's references to his war experiences are typically bitter: . . . "all those dead heroes on their benches in heaven, just heartsick

*THUNDER ROAD (1958). With son Jim Mitchum*

*THUNDER ROAD (1958). With Keely Smith*

for home. I'd be heartsick for home too, if I knew where it was." His remarks reflect his inability to readjust to civilian life.

In the film, Mitchum is pursued not only by government agents but also by a big-city syndicate, which is trying to take over the local whiskey trade. A rugged non-conformist, Mitchum even goes against the moonshiners' loose trade association by continuing to run whiskey after they stop.

Mitchum's independence is accompanied by a cynical distrust of others and a fierce, protective loyalty to his own family, especially to his younger brother (played by his son, James Mitchum). Caution makes Mitchum the valley's best whiskey runner. He has the fastest car and the most elaborate gadgetry (detachable bumpers, nail and oil spreaders) to enable him to elude pursuers. He double-checks gas and alcohol levels, making sure his whiskey tank is empty before returning home. At one point, he discovers the mistake of one attendant who has left a couple of drops of moonshine in his tank (enough for an arrest), looks hard and meanly at him and stuffs a cigarette in the man's mouth and lights it, expressing his anger through the violence of his gestures.

Mitchum's paranoia and his profession, which forces him to live by night, draw him further and further away from everyday life: in the film's most frequent image of Mitchum, he is alone driving his car down a dark country road. As Richard Thompson writes, "The film's haunting car sequences occur at night; moonlight, headlights, ghostly forms by the shoulders, the road itself fading in front and behind. This tiny microcosm formed by the radius of Mitchum's lights picking out for an instant a tunnel through blackness is the perfect metaphysical conceit for Mitchum's meaning in the film."*

As Thompson points out, the iconography of the road is crucial to the film's meaning. Life, for Mitchum, consists of racing down the road through the night, outwitting and outdistancing his pursuers. It is a life of speed and loneliness. It is not only a race against others but also a race against him-

* Richard Thompson, *Kings of the Bs*, New York: E.P. Dutton & Co., Inc. (1975), p. 212

self. Loss of control means death for Mitchum at the end of the film when he loses control, leaves the road at high speed and crashes into a roadside power plant.

The film's story and its images bring out the self-destructive aspects of Mitchum's persona. His inability to give up his way of life, in spite of his awareness that he is "due for a fall," reflects a passive acceptance of the consequences of his chosen way of life. Though he thunders down the highway in his car, Mitchum is the victim of his own inertia. Though he seems to be going somewhere, he is not.

*THE ANGRY HILLS (1959). With Gia Scala*

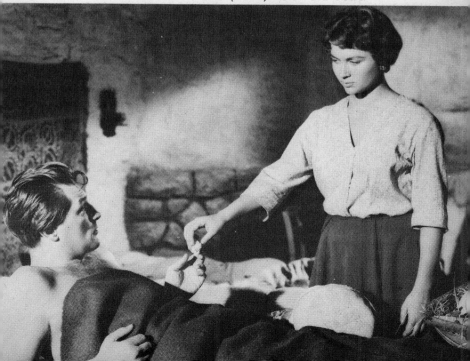

*THE WONDERFUL COUNTRY (1959). As Martin Brady*

In *The Angry Hills* (1959), chaotically directed by Robert Aldrich, Mitchum plays a cynical war correspondent, forcibly entrusted with a list of names of potential Allied agents in Nazi-occupied Greece. Mitchum's heroism is reluctant: the list is secretly passed to him after he refuses it, and his contact is killed before he can return it.

Forced to flee with the British to the hills when the Nazis take Athens, Mitchum is tracked by the Gestapo agent Stanley Baker, who wants the list of names. Mitchum fearfully participates in a guerrilla raid on a German supply camp, barely escaping with his life. All around him, patriotic Greeks sacrifice themselves for their country (and to save him), while he remains cynical and unconvinced. He tells the Greek mountain girl (Gia Scala) who nurses him back to health and whose family sacrifices their son to save him: "I've been around too much. There's not much left to believe in."

When he learns of the girl's murder by the Nazis, Mitchum telephones Baker, telling him he will kill him. Cynical patriot Sebastian Cabot prevents Mitchum from throwing away his life uselessly in an attempt to kill Baker and tells him that he can best serve Greece by delivering his important list to the British.

Mitchum's character makes little sense. He is impulsive, foolish, angry and sadistic. His conversion to idealistic patriotism lacks emotional force, and the film leaves his energy unfocused.

Mitchum produced *The Wonderful Country* (1959), and his participation left its stamp on the film, both in the character he plays and in the unconventional nature of the screenplay. Mitchum plays Martin Brady, an American expatriate and bodyguard for the Castros, a Mexican family presently in power. Mitchum's rootless adventurer is neither Mexican nor American: he is a man without a country.

The opening of the film, set on the edge of the Rio Grande, visually emphasizes Mitchum's ambivalent national identity. Sent by the Castros to buy guns in Texas, Mitchum and his men wait on the Mexican side of the river for their American contact. Bearded, his eyes heavy-lidded and his Mexican clothes dusty, Mitchum distrustfully peers out from under his sombrero at an approaching rider and speaks to his men with a thick Mexican accent. The dusty, barren landscape, the atmosphere and the situation, though objectively real and appropriate to the story, also function as extensions of the Mitchum persona and its archetypal predicament.

Though wanted by the police for killing his father's murderer in the United States, Mitchum accom-

*THE WONDERFUL COUNTRY (1959). With Leroy (Satchel) Paige*

panies his untrustworthy contact across the river, saying merely, "I want to see the other side." Mitchum's near-fatal curiosity suggests his discontentment with his life as it is. As in *The Lusty Men*, he appears to be looking for something he thinks he has lost. In Texas, Mitchum's horse, startled by tumbleweed, throws him, and he breaks his leg. In a very awkward but poetic scene that accentuates his alienation, townspeople gather around and look at him as he lies helpless in the street.

Mitchum's silence during the painful leg-setting reflects a stoicism that masks his inner sensitivity; one senses that he is constantly *feeling* his new experiences, as though remembering something

he had forgotten. He observes the behavior of those around him, his Mexican accent fades, replaced by a Texas drawl, and, after a comic public bath, he is given a set of American clothes by the friendly town doctor (Charles McGraw).

Regaining his American identity along with his native accent and new clothes, Mitchum finds there is a place for him in the community. The army major (Gary Merrill) asks his advice on a proposed pact between the army and the Castros to combine efforts against the Apaches. The captain of the local Texas Rangers knows of Mitchum's criminal past, but instead of arresting him, he offers to help clear him and asks him to join the rangers—if he can stay out of trouble. Though caught on the wrong side of the border, Mitchum's stay in Texas is more therapeutic than self-destructive.

Though instinctively drawn to trouble, Mitchum tries to avoid it, but it turns up in the form of the major's wife (Julie London). When Mitchum meets her, he gives her a long, hard look, indicating that he can immediately sense the unhappiness of her marriage, her loneliness, and her potential unfaithfulness. In the sort of brutally honest love scene that Mitchum does so well, he tells her that she is trouble and that he wants none of it, even though he is attracted to her. Shortly afterward, Mitchum nevertheless falls prey to his own uncontrollable character: he shoots the murderer of the German clerk who had befriended him, and he is again forced to flee to Mexico.

Mitchum's American experiences reform him, nonetheless. When Don Cipriano Castro orders him to kill his dangerous brother Marco, Mitchum refuses, saying that he no longer kills for money. He redeems himself with the Americans by guiding them safely past Marco's men and the Apaches, though Merrill is killed in the process. In the final scene, Mitchum stands alone on the edge of the Rio Grande. He lays down his gunbelt and sombrero on the Mexican side and wades across the river into Texas, returning to his own country in a final attempt to come to terms with the past he has always fled.

In *Home From the Hill* (1960), Mitchum gives the best performance of his career as Wade Hunnicutt, a despotic Texas land baron.

HOME FROM THE HILL (1960). With George Hamilton

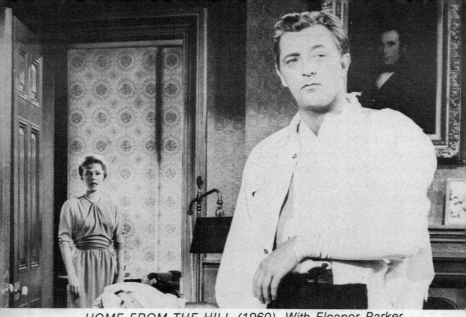

*HOME FROM THE HILL.* (1960). With Eleanor Parker

The film deals explicitly with the Mitchum persona, exploring it, testing its parameters, and finally reshaping it. Vincente Minnelli's melodrama gets beneath superficial images, uncovering complex personalities and releasing them from their stereotyped roles.

In at least a half-dozen pictures, Mitchum plays a hunter—of animals or of men. The opening sequence of *Home From the Hill* again exploits this metaphor, presenting Mitchum as the hunter who is shot at by an irate husband. Mitchum is a hunter who pursues not only game but women, and frequently "crosses other men's fences" to get them. Intent on getting what he wants, he observes few

rules and doesn't care whom he hurts. Mitchum's masculinity is defined by his pursuits: he hunts, chases women, gets drunk, and carouses with his male friends. His paneled den, filled with trophies, animal heads and horns, a bear rug, leather-upholstered chairs and a wood-burning fireplace, expresses his image of himself. But Mitchum is a prisoner of this self-image: it shuts him off from his wife, his son and from any real feeling; just as the decor of his room differs from that of the rest of the house, so he remains isolated within his private world.

Mitchum has a philosophy of hunting. He tells his son Theron (George Hamilton) that "What

104

every man hunts out there is himself." During the course of the picture, Mitchum changes from hunter to hunted, discovering his true self in the process. He fails in his attempts to establish a relationship with Hamilton and to turn him into a man made in his own image. Discarding his role as woman-chaser, he tries to make contact with his wife (Eleanor Parker), who has not slept with him during the eighteen years since she discovered that he fathered an illegitimate child (George Peppard) before their marriage. Though he talks gently and romantically to her, his charm does not work: she refuses to forgive him. Mitchum's desire to change meets with frustration: Hamilton, enraged at Mitchum's refusal to acknowledge Peppard, breaks with his father, and Parker, when Hamilton leaves home, has a nervous breakdown.

Mitchum's great resource is his strength. Convinced that the only way to win back Hamilton's love is to become worthy of it, he courageously proposes to his wife that they start all over again, building a new life. However, Mitchum's past image prevents him from creating a new one. Thinking that Mitchum is the father of his daughter's child, a neighbor (Everett Sloane) vows to kill him. Mitchum, flushed with pride that he could convince his wife to start again, opens a bottle of beer in his den and toasts the boar's head on the wall. As he fills his pipe, he

*THE NIGHT FIGHTERS (1960). With Richard Harris*

turns around, and Sloane kills him with a shotgun.

Ironically the father of the child is Mitchum's own son, Theron. This gives the story something of the force of a Greek tragedy; Mitchum cannot escape his past or his earlier self-image. The trap of personality snares Mitchum but not his sons, who finally free themselves from their self-images.

The Mitchum persona of a "man's man," firmly established at the beginning of the film, changes. Mitchum tries to act like a father to his son, patiently teaching him what he knows. This new sense of responsibility leads him to a reconciliation with his wife, further reinforcing his new identity as family man. Mitchum's honesty, directness and self-reliance give him admirable strength as he fights the stagnation that his previous country-gentleman way of life has imposed on him. Mitchum's discontent, his desire for change, emerges in *Home From the Hill* as a remarkably positive aspect of his personality. Yet it is not enough to free him from the trap of his own past failings.

Mitchum starred in *The Night Fighters* (1960), based on Arthur Roth's novel *A Terrible Beauty*. An unusually critical view of the IRA, the movie directly links the organization's activities during World War II to the Nazis, who supply the members with arms and training.

Mitchum plays Dermot O'Neill, a tough, ruggedly independent, heavy-drinking Irishman. Mitchum is unemployed and landless. As his girl Neeve (Anne Heywood) says, he is "thirty-five and still driftin'." Though he can hold his own in a fight, Mitchum has a soft, easy manner and gentle ways. His friends remark, "He'd rather joke a man out of his temper than take the trouble to raise his fists."

Reluctant to follow Heywood's suggestion that he go to England to find work, Mitchum is recruited by the IRA. His first mission, a raid on an armory, is easy and enjoyed. But after a bloody attack on a British power plant, during which Mitchum's Protestant friend Sean (Richard Harris) is wounded, he becomes disillusioned with the IRA, and his disillusionment grows when they do nothing to free Sean after he is caught. Mitchum's once-naive patriotism becomes more cynical; his dislike of the IRA's brutal methods brings him into conflict with the group, and he first turns informer to prevent them from killing innocent people on a proposed raid, and then quits the organization.

As part of the IRA, Mitchum had begun to lose his identity to that of the group. Always thriving in the role of the independent outsider, he leaves. For Mitchum, his friendship with Harris, his love for Heywood and his family, become

*THE GRASS IS GREENER (1960). With Cary Grant*

more important than the IRA's doubtful attempts to liberate Ireland. Mitchum discovers that political freedom begins with personal freedom, a notion basic to the anarchic Mitchum persona.

In 1960, Mitchum made two contrasting films with Deborah Kerr. In the first, *The Grass is Greener*, co-starring with Cary Grant, their teaming is awkward and inauspicious, sharing none of the ease and familiarity that characterizes their beautiful relationship in *The Sundowners*. Mitchum is miscast as a millionaire American tourist who aggressively bursts in on Kerr in the private rooms of her English castle, sweeping her off her feet and kissing her passionately. Mitchum,

though direct, forceful and honest in his love, is no match for Kerr's devious and clever husband (Cary Grant), who badgers Mitchum into a duel and wounds himself, leaving Mitchum unscathed. Grant's sacrificial wound regains the affections of his wife.

Mitchum was out of place in the genteel, drawing-room atmosphere of contemporary England. But he is very much at home in rugged Australian exteriors in the role of an itinerant sheep drover in *The Sundowners* (1960). Mitchum and his family are "the sundowners" of the title. As Mitchum's son Sean (Michael Anderson, Jr.) explains: "A sundowner is someone whose home is where the sun goes down.

It's someone who doesn't have a home." Mitchum's Paddy Carmody, a lower-class, hard-working Irishman, embodies all the contradictions of the archetypal pioneer: his rootlessness suggests a unique personal freedom, but his love and loyalty toward his family qualify this freedom with a freely chosen responsibility towards others. The power of Mitchum's performance in *The Sundowners* is due to the tension between the lonely drifter's love of freedom (a standard Mitchum trait) and his sense of responsibility as the loving father and husband, which gives meaning to his freedom.

Mitchum's love for the road comes into conflict with his love for his wife (Deborah Kerr) when Kerr decides that it is time to settle down and own a home. Instead of destroying the relationship between Mitchum and Kerr, however, this conflict simply demonstrates its durability. Kerr playfully nags Mitchum into taking a steady job and saving his pay. He does what she wants him to do, yet he remains independent, retaining both his rebelliousness and his masculinity. Mitchum senses that Kerr is as strong-willed as he is and respects her for it. As a result, he does not so much submit to her as emerge as her equal. The flexibility they share enables them to retain their dignity.

The film, which concentrates on small poetic moments rather than on epic issues, provides a lyrical setting for the exposition of their relationship. The intimacy between Mitchum and Kerr makes it clear that they are not only lovers but best friends, that they know one another as few couples on the screen do. As in *Heaven Knows, Mr. Allison*, they respect one another's uniqueness. Their differences are pronounced. The ambitionless Mitchum lives from day to day, spending money when he has it and never thinking about the future. Kerr dreams of a home and saves money in a jar, and, ashamed of the sympathetic looks that other women give her, she aspires to better things. Yet the earthy, comfortable reality of their relationship bridges these differences.

Mitchum's performances in *Home From the Hill* and *The Sundowners* earned him the National Board of Review's award as the best actor of 1960. Ironically, other actors had originally been cast for both parts: Clark Gable for *Home From the Hill* and Gary Cooper for *The Sundowners*. Their poor health gave Mitchum the opportunity to prove that, given a good role, he could match and even surpass the talent of any other actor in the business.

*THE SUNDOWNERS (1960). With Deborah Kerr*

During the sixties, Mitchum made a string of indifferent and inferior films. He accepted cameo roles in *The Longest Day* (1962), *The List of Adrian Messenger* (1963), and *What a Way to Go!* (1964) and supporting parts in *5 Card Stud* (1968) and *Secret Ceremony* (1969). He slept through *Villa Rides* (1968) and rounded out the decade with a pair of insipid western programmers, *Young Billy Young* (1969) and *The Good Guys and the Bad Guys* (1969). Poor judgment resulted in odd parts in off-beat, stagy movies like *Two For the Seesaw* (1962) and *Man in the Middle* (1964) or in a feeble farce like *The Last Time I Saw Archie* (1961). Mitchum's management of his career had always been lackadaisical but now it became dismally so. The only good films he made during the sixties were *Mister Moses* (1965) and *El Dorado* (1967).

One of Mitchum's better performances during this period was in *Cape Fear* (1962). The film was shot on location in Georgia, where Mitchum was technically in danger himself of being sent back to complete his sentence on a chain-gang from which he had escaped years earlier. Mitchum plays Max Cady, a sadistic ex-convict who terrorizes a lawyer (Gregory Peck) whose testimony sent him to jail. Mitchum's characterization of the sexual psychopath earns him a

# THE SIXTIES: NOT READY FOR INTEGRATION

prominent niche in the pantheon of screen villains. His performance captures the symptoms of the classical psychopath—total amorality and self-sufficiency to the point of alienation. Mitchum's acting is more gothic than realistic: he does not psychoanalyze or give the explicable motivation to Cady that would permit an audience to understand and, therefore, dismiss his villainy. His threatening late-night phone calls to Peck are clearly motivated; but he beats up a runaway girl for no reason at all, and threatens to kill her if she files a complaint. The Mitchum character is more chilling than other villains precisely because Mitchum plays him with sympathy, refusing as an actor to condemn the character he plays.

Mitchum's evil parallels his appearance: it is languorous and casual. He walks around in a shabby panama hat, his mouth holding a half-smoked cigar, a sinister sneer on his face. He is dressed in slacks and wears a short-sleeve shirt open at the collar, and his shirt-tails are not tucked in. This casual informality masks a vicious animal brutality: he tracks Peck's family to Cape Fear, breaks the neck of the

THE LONGEST DAY (1962). As Brig. General Cota

deputy guarding them, starts to rape Peck's wife, then goes after the daughter. Peck grapples with Mitchum in the river and after Mitchum half-nelsons him under the water, he breaks free and clubs him with a rock. Peck finally subdues Mitchum and, though tempted to kill him, restrains himself, realizing that prison is a more terrifying fate for Mitchum than death.

The casting of Peck and Mitchum as hero and villain is a study in extremes. Peck's intelligence and idealism give him nobility, social conscience, even self-righteousness. Like a good family man, he observes and enforces the law. The slovenly, brutal, unintelligent but crafty Mitchum breaks laws or uses them to aid him in his persecution of the law-abiding Peck. If Peck is superego, Mitchum is pure id.

Reviewers of *Two For the Seesaw* (1962) complained that Mitchum was miscast as Jerry Ryan, the unhappily married, indecisive Nebraska lawyer, romantically involved with a New York girl (Shirley MacLaine), and compared him unfavorably to Henry Fonda, who played the role on the stage. The film's faults, however, are more those of a turgid script and idiosyncratic direction than of poor acting. In fact, though he is oddly cast, Mitchum plays his part perfectly, capturing without condescension the pathos of the character's painful attempts to reach out and establish contact with another human being. Mitchum has played inert, indecisive, unemotional parts before, though rarely has he been forced to wallow in the

111

*CAPE FEAR (1962). With Polly Bergen*

sort of self-pity that characterizes his dialogue here.

*Rampage* (1963) builds a triangle of conflict and romance around big-game trapper Mitchum, trophy-hunter Jack Hawkins, and trophy Elsa Martinelli. The film opposes Mitchum, as "the catcher," against Hawkins, "the killer." A German zoo hires Mitchum and Hawkins to catch a rare animal called "the enchantress," half tiger and half leopard.

The film exploits but does not explore the contradictions of the Mitchum persona, contrasting his unheroic qualities—his nastiness, treachery, and lack of compassion for the failing powers of Hawkins—with his heroism in the hunt and his humanism in his relationship with the Malay guide, played by veteran Indian actor, Sabu. The film's climax is not in the ordeals of strength, endurance and courage undergone by Mitchum, but in his sad farewell to Sabu after the completion of the hunt: it is a leave-taking all the more moving in that it marks Sabu's last screen appearance.

In *Man in the Middle* (1964) Mitchum plays an army lawyer during World War II, ordered to defend the American murderer of a British officer. The army brass wants the man hanged in order to smooth out rocky British-American relations in India. Mitchum, discovering that the man (Keenan Wynn) is insane, is torn between his moral duty and his career. After equivocating for the greater part of the picture, Mitchum decides that "expediency can have no part in justice," and finally argues a plea of insanity that saves Wynn's life.

The film becomes a test of Mitchum's character, questioning the integrity that his earlier films assume. As Mitchum grows older, the carefree self-confidence and lonely iconoclasm apparent in his earlier performances have tended to yield to a need for the security and stability of a family or career, this need being more fully articulated in such later films as *Ryan's Daughter* (1970), *Going Home* (1972) and *The Friends of Eddie Coyle* (1973). *Man in the Middle* partially recognizes the changes that are taking place in the Mitchum persona, but never fully realizes them.

*Mister Moses* (1965) and *El Dorado* (1967) examine a different aspect of Mitchum's image and reveal the actor's great versatility. Mitchum's best films explore the dramatic aspects of his personality. *Out of the Past, Angel Face, The Lusty Men, Thunder Road* and *Home from the Hill* present Mitchum as a more or less anti-heroic, tragic figure whose past life or character destroy him. Yet

CAPE FEAR (1962).
As Max Cady

Mitchum's screen identity also has comic dimensions. Even in *Out of the Past*, Mitchum's irony reveals a comic potential. Unimaginative comedies like *The Grass is Greener* and *What a Way to Go!*, in which Mitchum played a cameo role as one of Shirley MacLaine's ill-fated husbands, do little with the actor but treat him as a good-natured, thick-headed bumpkin. The only films that realize the comic qualities inherent in the Mitchum persona are *Mister Moses* and *El Dorado*.

*Mister Moses*, in particular, brings out the kindness, generosity

113

TWO FOR THE SEESAW (1962). With Shirley MacLaine

TS-35/29-13

and sentimentality that lie beneath Mitchum's patina of cynicism and hard-boiled worldliness. His over-amiability and his difficulty in saying "no" become positive character traits—as well as the raw material for numerous comic scenes. Through an inversion of Mitchum's often satanic image, he becomes messianic; the distrustful loner turns into Joe Moses leading his people to the promised land.

Joe Moses is an African diamond smuggler, con-artist and medicine-show man. Like the earlier Moses, Mitchum is discovered floating downriver. He has been knocked unconscious by angry natives who have applied his miracle snake oil internally rather than externally, and he is rescued by the Masai tribe among the bull-rushes and taken to a hospital run by the local missionary's daughter Julie (Carroll Baker).

Slick, cynical and never at a loss for words, Mitchum presumptuously decides to win Baker, saying he "never had a girl named Julie before." Mitchum's cocktail party patter seems incongruous in the jungle, just as his Biblical quotations and references to Greek mythology seem incompatible with his carny-like character. With typical charm, Mitchum again plays an itinerant loner who seems to care about no one but himself. Yet his selfishness masks a selflessness which reluctantly reveals itself

when Baker cons the con-man into guiding the tribe, which must be re-located to make way for a reservoir, to their new home.

The semi-Christian Masai tribal chieftain believes that Mitchum, as another Moses, is the man to take his tribe and refuses to go unless Mitchum leads them. Baker uses the knowledge that Mitchum is a diamond smuggler to blackmail him into taking the job. (Mitchum mutters to Baker as he agrees: "It looks like I've been out-hustled.") The new Moses, singing "The Battle Hymn of the Republic," takes on the job of leading the tribe to their new home, good-naturedly enjoying rather than resenting his ironic role. Feeling more and more responsible and affectionate toward the tribe, he guides them safely to their destination. The British police, aware that he is a smuggler, order him to move on. Mitchum explains to the chief that he cannot stay. The chief asks, "You not come to promised land?" Mitchum tells him, "Well, chief, I guess they figure I'm not ready for integration." The chief: "Not understand, 'integration'?" Mitchum replies, "Well, you're not the only one, chief, believe me."

Mitchum's entanglements, though they begin superficially with an erotic interplay with Baker and end more profoundly with his temporary integration into a whole tribe, have a comic focal point in

*RAMPAGE (1963). With Elsa Martinelli and Jack Hawkins*

*MAN IN THE MIDDLE (1964). With Barry Sullivan*

his relationship with Emily, his elephant. Emily follows Mitchum around in spite of his advice that she "go back to Disneyland" or "go powder her nose." Mitchum's rapport with the elephant increases when she saves his life by crushing a snake about to bite him. Mitchum starts talking to Emily in Hindustani, riding her and training her to pull his sideshow wagon. At the end, the homeless, tribeless Mitchum walks off into the veldt with Emily, until Baker finally joins the odd-looking caravan.

*Mister Moses*, like most Mitchum-dominated films, has few artistic pretensions; such pretensions do not go with Mitchum's image. Its comic treatment of the Mitchum image, however, is more than entertainment; it reveals a new side of the actor's personality, a side that Howard Hawks explores more carefully and consistently in *El Dorado*.

Where Mitchum's humor in *Mister Moses* is chiefly verbal, in *El Dorado* it is largely slapstick. *Mister Moses* examines the intellectual aspects of Mitchum's comic potential; *El Dorado* takes a more physical approach. *El Dorado* explores the weaknesses in the Mitchum persona—his laziness, inertia, vulgarity, his clownishly

*MISTER MOSES (1965). As Joe Moses,*
*leading his charges to their new home*

apathetic lack of self-respect. Qualities that are treated seriously elsewhere become, in *El Dorado*, the subject of low comedy. Mitchum plays his part without the least trace of self-consciousness or irony, spoofing more than satirizing his own failings.

Mitchum plays aging sheriff J.P. Harrah, alongside John Wayne's aging gunfighter, Cole Thornton. Old friends and rivals, Mitchum and Wayne are equals and opposites. In the first scene, the two professionals, in a friendly matching of wits, test each other's competency and come to an amicable stand-off. Wayne, putting on his vest, moves toward his gun. Mitchum stops him. Wayne says: "I just wanted to

*MISTER MOSES (1965). With Carroll Baker*

see if you'd slowed down any."
Mitchum warily replies: "Not that
much."

Director Howard Hawks ex-
ploits the differences between
Wayne and Mitchum in a way that
makes *El Dorado* more a comedy
of character than of situation.
Wayne's moral and physical infallibility, even in old age, put him
among the effortless Olympians;
Mitchum, morally and physically
vulnerable, struggles just to keep
himself glued together. Mitchum
eventually does fall apart and
Wayne returns to town to help put
him back together. Many of the
film's slapstick comedy routines
stem from the interplay between the
independent, ornery Mitchum, who
refuses to be helped, and Wayne,
who insists on helping, at least from

*EL DORADO (1967). With Arthur Hunnicutt and John Wayne*

a respectful distance.

In one scene, Wayne throws a pail of water on Mitchum and rouses him from his jail-cell cot. Unshaven, dirty and hung-over, wearing a tattered red undershirt that accentuates his paunch, the sub-human Mitchum laboriously sits up, tries to focus his bleary eyes, and snarls a few words at Wayne. Using Wayne's hand to get to his feet, Mitchum comes up swinging, and Wayne crowns him with a handy spittoon. Mitchum's eyes grow glassy, his body stiffens, and he topples back onto his cot. Wayne, aided by his friends, pour a home-made remedy down Mitchum's throat to sober him up. Reacting with his whole body, Mitchum stiffens, then convulses as the concoction takes effect. The

*EL DORADO (1967). With John Wayne*

crude humor of these scenes reflects the zero level of humanity to
which Mitchum has fallen; he has
become pure brute force.

Mitchum continues to battle with
his physical infirmities—he fumbles
with guns, gunbelts and
bullets—but his professional competence slowly returns. He trails a
gunman to a saloon and, in a scene
that recalls his first encounter with

Wayne, spots an unfriendly bar-
tender (played by Mitchum's
brother John) reaching for a gun
and stops him, giving him a bloody
handful of splinters in the process.
As Mitchum begins to regain his
lost dignity, Hawks celebrates the
event by constructing a comic scene
around the violation of that dignity.
As Mitchum takes a much-needed
bath, all of his friends bring him

*THE WAY WEST (1967). With Kirk Douglas*

bars of soap. An old mutual girl-friend (Charlene Holt) of Mitchum and Wayne pays a call, and Mitchum remarks that there is "more privacy in the middle of the El Paso railway station." When Holt leaves the jail, she walks past the bathing Mitchum, who salvages what little dignity he can by closing his own eyes as she passes.

Mitchum's struggle to regain control of his body—he continues to double over in pain and clutch his convulsing stomach—lacks the seriousness of Dean Martin's similar attempts to achieve self-control in Hawks' *Rio Bravo*

(1959), partly because Mitchum, unlike Martin, is merely regaining the position of competence and control he holds at the film's beginning and partly because Mitchum's rehabilitation has none of the pressing inner necessity that characterizes Martin's. Mitchum makes mistakes, but he lives through them. Like Wayne, Mitchum is at peace with himself, though his peace is much less demanding than Wayne's. *El Dorado* uncovers the comic durability that Mitchum's apathy conceals.

Mitchum made a number of other westerns after *El Dorado*

*VILLA RIDES* (1968). Waiting on the set

*5 CARD STUD (1968). With Dean Martin*

(which was completed in 1966 but not released until 1967); none was as good as *El Dorado*, and they did little to advance his career. In *The Way West* (1967), Mitchum serves as guide for Kirk Douglas' wagon train, taking it from Missouri to Oregon. Mitchum, more tolerant and understanding of human failings than the autocratic Douglas, remains a whimsical outsider, observing the soap-operatics of the settlers from a cool distance, and he rejects white society at the end for life among the Blackfeet Indians. In *Villa Rides* (1968), Mitchum does little but exhale heavily as an American airplane pilot selling guns to the Mexican Army, who is captured and conscripted by Pancho Villa. Mercenary, coward-

ly, fat and complacent, Mitchum reveals a moral ambiguity here matched only by that in *Anzio* (1967). In *5 Card Stud* (1968) Mitchum is a fire-and-brimstone preacher who practices what he preaches: he demonically dispenses justice and takes vengeance, using a derringer concealed in his Bible. Mitchum sings the title song of *Young Billy Young* (1969) and plays the part of experienced lawman Ben Kane, who takes young gunslinger Billy Young (Robert Walker) under his wing. He reforms badman Walker, who reminds him of his son. Mitchum and Walker then spend the rest of the movie trying to prevent each other from acting rashly. In *The Good Guys and the Bad Guys* (1969),

Mitchum's aging sheriff teams up with an old outlaw crony (George Kennedy) to foil a train robbery.

Mitchum's other major roles in the sixties were in *Anzio* (1967) and *Secret Ceremony* (1969). In *Anzio*, Mitchum plays a skeptical American war correspondent who discovers, after the Anzio landing, that the Nazis have left the area undefended. The American general, suspecting a trap, orders his army to dig in, giving the Germans time to build their defenses.

More cynical than Ernie Pyle, Mitchum's correspondent speaks of war as "the ultimate game." To him, all wars are the same: "Men kill each other because they like to." Mitchum, as an impartial observer, is out of place on the bat-tlefield. Men in his ranger patrol die protecting him as he watches helplessly. Symbolically, he hides behind the body of a dead soldier during one attack. Mitchum's experiences prove that it is impossible to "observe" a war—that war does not permit rational neutrality. But the film refuses to take a clear-cut stand either on the military blunders that made a blood bath at Anzio or on the questionable pacifism of the Mitchum character. Like Mitchum's performance, it is a film of compromises.

Mitchum, bearded and wearing a raincoat, plays a dirty old man in Joseph Losey's *Secret Ceremony*. A cynical English college teacher, Mitchum returns from Phila-

*YOUNG BILLY YOUNG (1969). As Kane*

*ANZIO (1967). With Earl Holliman*

delphia, where his girl students called him "the wretched lecher," to London, unaware that his estranged wife has died and that his stepdaughter (Mia Farrow) has adopted a blowsy prostitute (Elizabeth Taylor) as a new mother. Mitchum's baroque performance suits the film's style. Vaguely sinister and sexually threatening, Mitchum stalks around the periphery of the Taylor-Farrow relationship, unwittingly becoming caught up in its complications: Farrow finally disowns her adopted mother and commits suicide. Taylor, blaming Mitchum for Farrow's death, kills him at the girl's funeral.

Losey's bitterly ironic film reveals the chaotic and self-destructive qualities the family can sometimes display. The three-way relationship of "father," "mother" and "daughter" has no exit. The imagined bond between Taylor and Farrow finally prevails, and Mitchum becomes the helpless victim of their secret ceremony.

*SECRET CEREMONY (1969). As Albert*

In recent years, the Mitchum persona has undergone changes. The characters he plays are more conservative. Rather than searching for something they had lost, they are trying to hold on to something they know they have. Mitchum's bitter cynicism has mellowed with age; he has become a man of patience and inner strength. His earlier lack of ambition has yielded to the security of a career and the responsibility of a family. Yet Mitchum's loyalties are individual rather than institutional. Though somewhat established himself, he remains anti-Establishment, continuing to exist on the fringe of society. Mitchum, no matter how conservative his parts, will always be subversive.

David Lean's *Ryan's Daughter* (1970) threatens to turn Mitchum into a speck on the landscape, but he surprisingly dominates the film by understating his character. The melodramatic, even hammy, performances of Sarah Miles, Christopher Jones, Leo McKern and John Mills match Lean's over-blown visual style, leaving Mitchum alone at the firm center which holds the film together.

Mitchum plays widower-school teacher Charles Shaughnessy, a soft-spoken, clumsy man whose chief pleasures are listening to Beethoven's Fifth Symphony on his victrola and collecting flowers, then cataloging and pressing them into

# THE FRIENDS OF ROBERT MITCHUM

books. Mitchum's middle-aged, sexually inadequate, fatherly teacher is mis-matched with the young, passionate and foolish Rosy Ryan (Sarah Miles), whose infidelities with a wounded, shell-shocked British officer (Christopher Jones) he patiently overlooks, hoping that the young couple's affair will burn itself out and that his wife will return to him. He stands by her when the townspeople accuse her of being an informer and, after Jones' suicide, leaves town with her.

Mitchum's attempts to underplay his part are partly frustrated by Lean's heavy-handed graphics: Mitchum sees two pairs of footprints in the sand—those of a woman and of a man with a limp. As Mitchum conceals his thoughts and stoically restrains his feelings, Lean inserts an imagined flashback in which Mitchum sees his wife and the British officer walking together on the beach. Lean's images and Maurice Jarre's musical crescendoes drown out Mitchum's quiet subtlety. Mitchum's understanding patience with Miles, though superficially an extension of their student-teacher relationship, reveals a tolerance of human frailty that stems from an awareness of his own imperfections and reflects the

*RYAN'S DAUGHTER (1970). With Sarah Miles*

transformation of his passivity from a negative into a positive virtue. The apathetic lack of concern that characterizes Mitchum's earlier roles has grown into a worldly forbearance in *Ryan's Daughter.*

In *Going Home* (1972), Mitchum plays ex-convict Harry Graham who, after going to prison for the murder of his wife, tries to re-establish a relationship with his son (Jan-Michael Vincent). Vincent's moody and erratic behavior tries Mitchum's fatherly patience, complicating his attempts to observe the conditions of his parole and to live peacefully with his girlfriend

Brenda Vaccaro. Mitchum's sympathetic, guiltless portrayal of Graham gives the character a quiet dignity that contrasts with Vincent's nervous and traumatized adolescent. When Vincent rapes Vaccaro in a scene heavily cut by MGM (who also cut Sylvia Miles' housewife completely out of the picture), Mitchum, recalling Max Cady in *Cape Fear,* savagely stalks Vincent in the woods outside their old home. However, he regains his self-control before committing a second murder. Mitchum's sense of responsibility to Vincent, tested to the breaking point, finally cedes to

*RYAN'S DAUGHTER (1970). As Charles Shaughnessy*

a more responsible self-concern. Mitchum's patient tolerance in *Going Home* reveals an inner strength around which he and Vaccaro can build a new life.

In *The Wrath of God* (1972), Mitchum plays priest Oliver Van Horne, excommunicated for protesting church corruption, who, in his cassock and hat, has become a con-man adventurer in Mexico. He carries a machine-gun in one suitcase and 53,000 ill-gotten dollars in another. As in *5 Card Stud*, he conceals a hand gun in his Bible, and his cross is a switchblade.

Cynical, foul-mouthed, lecherous and hypocritical, Mitchum is blackmailed into assassinating petty Mexican dictator Frank Langella. As part of his disguise, he performs priestly functions, holding Mass, hearing confessions, baptizing and marrying local peasants. Mitchum's priestly sense of responsibility gives his character an authenticity and sincerity that it lacks in earlier versions of the role (*Night of the Hunter, 5 Card Stud*).

The film's improbable conclusion has Mitchum, tortured and tied to a stone crucifix, kill Langella by toppling over the cross and crushing him with it. *The Wrath of God* gives Mitchum's brutality divine sanction and serves as an indication of how "respectable" Mitchum's unorthodox behavior has become.

In *The Friends of Eddie Coyle* (1973) Mitchum plays Coyle, an aging loser, an expendable middle man who exists on the fringe of the criminal world, supplying guns and (apparently) transporting stolen goods. He uses other people and is used in turn. He is expected to do a job, and, if he slips up, he can count on getting his knuckles broken, being betrayed, or getting killed.

At one point Mitchum gets to describe the character he plays. Looking haggard and weary, Mitchum becomes annoyed with the inexperience and youth of the person who sells him guns. Standing in a bowling alley while still chewing on some food, Mitchum, in his best Boston accent, tells him: "Look, I'm gettin' old, ya hear? I spend most of my life hangin' around crummy joints with a bunch of punks, drinkin' the beer, eatin' the hash and the hot dogs and watchin' the other people go off to Florida while I'm sweatin' out how I'm gonna pay the plumber. I done time when I stood up, but I can't take no more chances. Next time, it's gonna be me goin' to Florida. . . ."

Mitchum struggles to survive—not only in the treacherous underworld but outside. When caught with an illegal truckload of liquor, he becomes the fall-guy, taking the rap when he refuses to betray others. Mitchum plea bargains by providing information about criminal activities to the

GOING HOME (1972). With Brenda Vaccaro

police. Loyal to no one but himself, he betrays the man beneath
him (the gun runner), and, when
that fails to get him an acquittal, he
turns in the men he works for (the
bank robbers), not knowing that
they have already been betrayed by
another. He tries to work both ends
against the middle, but he fails and
is caught in the middle himself.
Characteristically, Mitchum is one

step behind his opponents: he is not
smart enough, fast enough or ruthless enough to survive the treachery of others.

*Eddie Coyle* investigates the
treacherous, self-protective nature
of the Mitchum image. *The Yakuza*
(1975) looks at another side of
Mitchum, exploring the positive
aspects of his sense of loyalty and
responsibility.

The film deals with ties of friendship and family. Ex-detective Harry Kilmer (Mitchum) helps his old war buddy Brian Keith retrieve his daughter who has been kidnapped in Japan by a *yakuza* gang. (A *yakuza*, which literally means "gambler," is a Japanese criminal who lives by a strict code of duty and honor).

Mitchum gets caught up in a complex system of loyalties and obligations. On arriving in Japan, he visits an old occupation girlfriend named Eiko (Kishi Keiko) and enlists the aid of her brother (Takakura Ken), a former *yakuza*, who is indebted to Mitchum for saving the lives of his sister and her daughter during the war. Mitchum discovers that Takakura is, in fact, Eiko's husband, and that his affair with her violated a Japanese code and destroyed her marriage. This knowledge puts Mitchum in Takakura's debt, climaxing in a rather ludicrously played scene in which Mitchum, observing the *yakuza* code, apologizes to the wronged Takakura by cutting off his own finger.

The softening of Mitchum's cynicism and his growing concern for his obligations to others that take

*THE WRATH OF GOD (1972). With Frank Langella*

*THE FRIENDS OF EDDIE COYLE (1973). In the title role*

*THE FRIENDS OF EDDIE COYLE (1973). With Steven Keats*

place in the seventies give Mitchum a credibility in *The Yakuza* that he would not have had a decade earlier.

Mitchum was next cast by Otto Preminger for the leading role in *Rosebud* (1975). Mitchum, who has never been able to make more than two pictures with any one director (Wellman fired him from *Blood Alley*, their third together), was fired by Preminger and was replaced by Peter O'Toole. After the *Rosebud* fiasco, Mitchum returned to Hollywood where he was cast as Philip Marlowe in a remake of Raymond Chandler's *Farewell, My Lovely* (1975). In the film, Mitchum is hired by recently paroled Moose Malloy (Jack O'Halloran) to find his former girlfriend, Velma (Charlotte Rampling). Velma, now married to a wealthy and powerful Los Angeles judge, doesn't want to be found and Mitchum, used by both O'Halloran and Rampling, is caught in the middle: he gets knocked uncon-

*THE YAKUZA (1975). With Takakura Ken*

scious, beaten up, shot full of dope, and fired at. Mitchum's Marlowe is vulnerable and not too smart. He serves chiefly as a catalyst to the actions of others; the case solves itself when those involved in it kill one another. Mitchum himself survives not through his own wits, like Bogart's Marlowe in *The Big Sleep* (1946), but through the timely intercession of the police.

Mitchum's Marlowe, unlike Chandler's, is not hard-boiled; he is neither tough nor cynical. Closer in spirit to Ross Macdonald's Lew Archer character, Mitchum is lonely, compassionate and sentimental. In one scene, he joins an aging, alcoholic ex-showgirl (Sylvia Miles) in a song, and at the end of the film he goes off to console the wife and child of a musician killed during the case.

Like *Murder, My Sweet* (a 1945

*FAREWELL, MY LOVELY (1975). As Philip Marlowe*

FAREWELL, MY LOVELY (1975). Marlowe is quizzed by the police.

version of the Chandler mystery starring Dick Powell), *Farewell, My Lovely* is told in flashback to capture the first-person subjectivity of Chandler's story. But Mitchum's compassionate concern for the characters around him undercuts Marlowe's egotism. Mitchum's references to himself deal primarily with his age and his weariness, giving his character a reflective mellowness which Chandler's detective lacks. Mitchum's Marlowe has a world-weary tolerance of human failings, a tolerance prompted by an awareness of his own fallibility. As a result, he is less moralistic and more sympathetic towards others. Mitchum softens Marlowe's worldly sensibility with an unworldly sensitivity, giving an emotional dimension to the character that previous screen Marlowes either ignored or failed to realize.

Mitchum has recently been cast in the Richard Zanuck and David Brown production of *The Battle of Midway*. As Mitchum tells Chicago *Sun-Times* interviewer Roger Ebert, "They wanted me to play General Fletcher. Ten weeks work. 'Sorry,' I said. 'I can't spare the time.' Then they have a role that's five weeks long. That's too long, too. Finally they call me up and offer me a role as Bull Halsey. 'How long?' I ask. 'One day,' they say, 'and he's in a hospital bed.' 'I can just about handle that,' I said."

Most film actors are just so much raw material which writers, producers and directors shape into characters. They are tools designed to perform a certain task, and occasionally they leave distinctive marks on the finished work. Robert Mitchum, unlike most actors, has shaped his own screen image, yet his management of his own career has been chaotic and what might flatteringly be called "courageously experimental." His best films are those in which his persona has been intelligently explored by others or in which he was personally involved as producer or writer.

What distinguishes Mitchum from other major stars is that he changes, constantly eluding categorization. Mitchum continues to grow within his craft, renewing himself with each role. Tough and vulnerable, cynical and sentimental, heroic and anti-heroic, Mitchum embodies many contradictory qualities. He remains an enigmatic anarchist.

# BIBLIOGRAPHY

Agee, James, *Agee on Film,* Beacon Press, Boston, 1958.

Byron, Stuart, "On a Clear Day You Can See Minnelli," *December,* vol. XV (1973).

Cameron, Ian and Elisabeth, *Dames*, Praeger, New York, 1969.

Garnett, Tay, *Light Up Your Torches and Pull Up Your Tights,* Arlington House, New York, 1973.

Macdonald, Ross, *On Crime Writing,* Capra Press, Santa Barbara, 1973.

Miller, Don, *"B" Movies,* Curtis Books, New York, 1973.

Minnelli, Vincente (with Hector Arce), *I Remember It Well*, Doubleday and Co., New York, 1974.

Ringgold, Gene, "Robert Mitchum," *Films in Review,* May 1964.

Shipman, David, *The Great Movie Stars,* St. Martin's Press, New York, 1972.

Thompson, Richard, "Thunder Road: Maudit — 'The Devil Got Him First'," *Kings of the Bs* (ed. T. McCarthy and C. Flynn), E.P. Dutton & Co., New York, 1975.

*The Thousand Eyes*, vol. 3 (Raoul Walsh issue), June 1974.

Tomkies, Mike, *The Robert Mitchum Story,* Ballantine Books, New York, 1973.

*The Velvet Light Trap,* no. 10 (RKO issue), Fall 1973.

Wellman, William, *A Short Time For Insanity,* Hawthorn Books, New York, 1974.

Wood, Robin, "Night of the Hunter/Novel Into Film," *On Film,* no. 1, 1970.

# THE FILMS OF ROBERT MITCHUM

*The director's name follows the release date. A (c) following the release date indicates that the film was in color. Sp indicates Screenplay and b/o indicates based/on.*

1. HOPPY SERVES A WRIT. United Artists, 1943. *George Archainbaud.* Sp: Gerald Geraghty, b/o novel by Clarence E. Mulford. Cast: William Boyd, Andy Clyde, Jay Kirby, Victor Jory, George Reeves, Jan Christy.

2. THE LEATHER BURNERS. United Artists, 1943. *Joseph Henabery.* Sp: Jo Pagano, b/o novel by Bliss Lomax and characters created by Clarence E. Mulford. Cast: William Boyd, Jay Kirby, Andy Clyde, Shelly Spencer.

3. BORDER PATROL. United Artists, 1943. *Lesley Selander.* Sp: Michael Wilson, b/o characters created by Clarence E. Mulford. Cast: William Boyd, Andy Clyde, Jay Kirby, Claudia Drake, Russell Simpson, Duncan Renaldo, George Reeves.

4. FOLLOW THE BAND. Universal, 1943. *Jean Yarbrough.* Sp: Warren Wilson and Dorothy Bennett, b/o story by Richard English. Cast: Leon Errol, Mary Beth Hughes, Eddie Quillan, Skinnay Ennis, Anne Rooney, Samuel S. Hinds, Ben Bartlett.

5. COLT COMRADES. United Artists, 1943. *Lesley Selander.* Sp: Michael Wilson, b/o characters created by Clarence E. Mulford. Cast: William Boyd, Andy Clyde, Jay Kirby, George Reeves, Gayle Lord, Victor Jory.

6. THE HUMAN COMEDY. MGM, 1943. *Clarence Brown.* Sp: Howard Estabrook, b/o story by William Saroyan (whose novel was published in conjunction with the film's release). Cast: Mickey Rooney, James Craig, Frank Morgan, Fay Bainter, Marsha Hunt, Van Johnson, Donna Reed.

7. WE'VE NEVER BEEN LICKED. Wanger-Universal, 1943. *John Rawlins.* Sp: Norman Reilly Raine and Nick Grinde. Cast: Richard Quine, Noah Beery, Jr., Anne Gwynne, Martha O'Driscoll, Samuel S. Hinds, Harry Davenport.

8. BEYOND THE LAST FRONTIER. Republic, 1943. *Howard Bretherton.* Sp: John K. Butler and Morton Grant. Cast: Eddie Dew, Smiley Burnette, Lorraine Miller, Richard Clarke, Harry Woods, Kermit Maynard.

9. BAR 20. United Artists, 1943. *Lesley Selander.* Sp: Mortimer Grant, Norman Houston and Michael Wilson. Cast: William Boyd, Andy Clyde, George Reeves, Dustin Farnum, Victor Jory, Douglas Fowley.

10. DOUGHBOYS IN IRELAND. Columbia, 1943. *Lew Landers.* Sp: Howard J. Green. Cast: Kenny Baker, Jeff Donnell, Lynn Merrick, Guy Bonham, Red Latham.

11. CORVETTE K-225. Universal, 1943. *Richard Rosson.* Sp: Lt. John Rhodes Sturdy. Cast: Randolph Scott, James Brown, Ella Raines, Barry Fitzgerald, Andy Devine, Richard Lane, Walter Sande.

12. THE LONE STAR TRAIL. Universal, 1943. *Ray Taylor.* Sp: Victor Halperin. Cast: Johnny Mack Brown, Tex Ritter, Fuzzy Knight, Jennifer Holt, George Eldredge, Harry Strang.

13. FALSE COLORS. United Artists, 1943. *George Archainbaud.* Sp: Bennett Cohen, b/o characters created by Clarence E. Mulford. Cast: William Boyd, Andy Clyde, Jimmy Rogers, Tom Seidel, Claudia Drake, Douglass Dumbrille.

14. THE DANCING MASTERS. 20th Century-Fox, 1943. *Mal St. Clair.* Sp: W. Scott Darling. Cast: Stan Laurel, Oliver Hardy, Trudy Marshall, Robert Bailey, Matt Briggs, Margaret Dumont, Allan Lane.

15. RIDERS OF THE DEADLINE. United Artists, 1943. *Lesley Selander.* Sp: Bennett Cohen, b/o characters created by Clarence E. Mulford. Cast: William Boyd, Andy Clyde, Jimmy Rogers, Richard Crane, Frances Woodward, Tony Ward.

16. GUNG HO! Wanger-Universal, 1943. *Ray Enright.* Sp: Lucien Hubbard, b/o story by Lt. W.S. Le Francois, U.S.M.C. Cast: Randolph Scott, Grace McDonald, Alan Curtis, Noah Beery, Jr., J. Carrol Naish, David Bruce, Peter Coe, Richard Lane.

17. JOHNNY DOESN'T LIVE HERE ANYMORE. Monogram, 1944. *Joe May*. Sp: Philip Yordan and John Kafka, b/o novel by Alice Means Reeve. Cast: James Ellison, Simone Simon, William Terry, Minna Gombell, Chick Chandler, Alan Dinehart, Gladys Blake.

18. WHEN STRANGERS MARRY. Monogram, 1944. *William Castle*. Sp: Philip Yordan and Dennis Cooper. Cast: Dean Jagger, Kim Hunter, Neil Hamilton, Lou Lubin, Milton Kibbee, Dewey Robinson.

19. THE GIRL RUSH. RKO, 1944. *Gordon Douglas*. Sp: Robert E. Kent, b/o story by Laszlo Vadnay and Aladar Laszlo. Cast: Wally Brown, Alan Carney, Frances Langford, Vera Vague (Barbara Jo Allen), Paul Hurst, Patti Brill.

20. THIRTY SECONDS OVER TOKYO. MGM, 1944. *Mervyn LeRoy*. Sp: Dalton Trumbo, b/o book by Capt. Ted W. Lawson and Robert Considine. Cast: Van Johnson, Robert Walker, Spencer Tracy, Phyllis Thaxter, Tim Murdock, Scott McKay, Don DeFore.

21. NEVADA. RKO, 1944. *Edward Killy*. Sp: Norman Houston, b/o novel by Zane Grey. Cast: Anne Jeffreys, Guinn "Big Boy" Williams, Nancy Gates, Richard Martin, Craig Reynolds. Also filmed in 1927 and 1935.

22. WEST OF THE PECOS. RKO, 1945. *Edward Killy*. Sp: Norman Houston, b/o novel by Zane Grey. Cast: Barbara Hale, Richard Martin, Thurston Hall, Rita Corday, Russell Hopton, Bill Williams, Bruce Edwards. Also filmed in 1934.

23. THE STORY OF G.I. JOE. Cowan-United Artists, 1945. *William A. Wellman*. Sp: Leopold Atlas, Guy Endore and Philip Stevenson, b/o newspaper articles of Ernie Pyle. Cast: Burgess Meredith, Freddie Steele, Wally Cassell, Jimmy Lloyd, Jack Reilly.

24. TILL THE END OF TIME. RKO, 1946. *Edward Dmytryk*. Sp: Allen Rivkin, b/o novel by Niven Busch *(They Dream of Home)*. Cast: Dorothy McGuire, Guy Madison, Bill Williams, Tom Tully, William Gargan, Jean Porter, Johnny Sands.

25. UNDERCURRENT. MGM, 1946. *Vincente Minnelli*. Sp: Edward Chorodov, b/o novel by Thelma Strabel *(You Were There)*. Cast: Katharine Hepburn, Robert Taylor, Edmund Gwenn, Marjorie Main, Jayne Meadows, Clinton Sundberg.

26. THE LOCKET. RKO, 1946. *John Brahm.* Sp: Sheridan Gibney. Cast: Laraine Day, Brian Aherne, Gene Raymond, Sharyn Moffett, Ricardo Cortez, Henry Stephenson, Katherine Emery.

27. PURSUED. Warner Bros., 1947. *Raoul Walsh.* Sp: Niven Busch. Cast: Teresa Wright, Judith Anderson, Dean Jagger, John Rodney, Harry Carey, Jr., Alan Hale.

28. CROSSFIRE. RKO, 1947. *Edward Dmytryk.* Sp: John Paxton, b/o novel by Richard Brooks *(The Brick Foxhole).* Cast: Robert Young, Robert Ryan, Gloria Grahame, Paul Kelly, George Cooper.

29. DESIRE ME. MGM, 1947. *George Cukor* (uncredited) and *Mervyn Le Roy.* Sp: Marguerite Roberts and Zoe Akins, b/o novel by Leonard Frank *(Karl and Anna).* Cast: Greer Garson, Richard Hart, George Zucco, Morris Ankrum, Florence Bates, Richard Humphreys.

30. OUT OF THE PAST. RKO, 1947. *Jacques Tourneur.* Sp: Geoffrey Homes (Daniel Mainwaring), b/o his novel *(Build My Gallows High).* Cast: Jane Greer, Kirk Douglas, Rhonda Fleming, Richard Webb, Steve Brodie, Paul Valentine, Virginia Huston, Dickie Moore.

31. RACHEL AND THE STRANGER. RKO, 1948. *Norman Foster.* Sp: Waldo Salt, b/o story by Howard Fast. Cast: Loretta Young, William Holden, Gary Gray, Tom Tully, Sara Haden.

32. BLOOD ON THE MOON. RKO, 1948. *Robert Wise.* Sp: Lillie Hayward and Harold Shumate, b/o novel by Luke Short. Cast: Barbara Bel Geddes, Robert Preston, Phyllis Thaxter, Walter Brennan, Frank Faylen, Tom Tully, Charles McGraw, Tom Tyler.

33. THE RED PONY. Republic, 1949 (c). *Lewis Milestone.* Sp: John Steinbeck, b/o his short stories. Cast: Myrna Loy, Louis Calhern, Shepperd Strudwick, Peter Miles, Margaret Hamilton. Remade as a television movie in 1973.

34. THE BIG STEAL. RKO, 1949. *Don Siegel.* Sp: Geoffrey Homes (Daniel Mainwaring) and Gerald Drayson Adams, b/o story by Richard Wormser. Cast: Jane Greer, William Bendix, Patric Knowles, Ramon Novarro, Don Alvarado, Pascual Garcia Pena, John Qualen.

35. HOLIDAY AFFAIR. RKO, 1949. *Don Hartman.* Sp: Isobel Lennart. Cast: Janet Leigh, Wendell Corey, Gordon Gebert, Griff Barnett, Esther Dale, Henry O'Neill, Henry Morgan.

36.   WHERE  DANGER  LIVES.  RKO,  1950.  *John Farrow.*  Sp:  Charles Bennett,  b/o  story  by  Leo  Rosten.  Cast:  Faith  Domergue,  Claude  Rains, Maureen  O'Sullivan,  Charles  Kemper,  Harry  Shannon,  Ralph  Dumke,  Billy House,  Philip  Van  Zandt,  Jack  Kelly,  Lillian  West.

37.   MY  FORBIDDEN  PAST.  RKO,  1951.  *Robert Stevenson.*  Sp:  Marion Parsonnet,  Leopold  Atlas,  b/o  novel  by  Polan  Banks  *(Carriage Entrance).*  Cast: Ava  Gardner,  Melvyn  Douglas,  Janis  Carter,  Lucile  Watson,  Basil  Ruysdael, Gordon  Oliver.

38.   HIS KIND OF WOMAN. RKO, 1951. *John Farrow.* Sp: Frank Fenton and Jack  Leonard.  Cast:  Jane  Russell,  Vincent  Price,  Tim  Holt,  Charles  McGraw, Raymond  Burr,  Marjorie  Reynolds,  Leslye  Banning,  Jim  Backus,  Philip  Van Zandt.

39.   THE  RACKET.  RKO,  1951.  *John Cromwell.*  Sp:  William  Wister  Haines and  W.R.  Burnett,  b/o  play  by  Bartlett  Cormack.  Cast:  Lizabeth  Scott,  Robert Ryan,  William  Talman,  Ray  Collins,  Joyce  MacKenzie,  Robert  Hutton,  Walter Sande.  Previously  filmed  in  1928.

40.   MACAO.  RKO,  1952.  *Josef von Sternberg.*  Sp:  Bernard  C.  Schoenfeld and  Stanley  Rubin.  Cast:  Jane  Russell,  William  Bendix,  Thomas  Gomez,  Gloria Grahame,  Brad  Dexter,  Edward  Ashley,  Philip  Ahn,  Vladimir  Sokoloff.

41.   ONE  MINUTE  TO  ZERO.  RKO,  1952.  *Tay Garnett.*  Sp:  Milton  Krims and  William  Wister  Haines.  Cast:  Ann  Blyth,  William  Talman,  Charles McGraw,  Margaret  Sheridan,  Richard  Egan.

42.   THE  LUSTY  MEN.  RKO,  1952.  *Nicholas Ray.*  Sp:  Horace  McCoy  and David  Dortort,  b/o  story  by  Claude  Stanush.  Cast:  Susan  Hayward,  Arthur Kennedy,  Arthur  Hunnicutt,  Frank  Faylen,  Walter  Coy,  Carol  Nugent,  Maria Hart,  Lorna  Thayer.

43.   ANGEL  FACE.  RKO,  1952.  *Otto Preminger.*  Sp:  Frank  Nugent and  Oscar Millard.  Cast:  Jean  Simmons,  Mona  Freeman,  Herbert  Marshall,  Leon  Ames, Barbara  O'Neill,  Kenneth  Tobey,  Raymond  Greenleaf.

44.   WHITE  WITCH  DOCTOR.  20th  Century-Fox,  1953  (c).  *Henry Hathaway.*  Sp:  Ivan  Goff  and  Ben  Roberts,  b/o  novel  by  Louise  A.  Stinedorf. Cast:  Susan  Hayward,  Walter  Slezak,  Mashood  Ajala,  Joseph  C.  Norcisse, Elzie  Emanuel,  Timothy  Carey.

45. SECOND CHANCE. RKO, 1953 (c). *Rudolph Mate.* Sp: Oscar Millard and Sidney Boehm. Cast: Linda Darnell, Jack Palance, Sandro Giglio, Rodolfo Hoyos, Jr., Reginald Sheffield.

46. SHE COULDN'T SAY NO. RKO, 1954. *Lloyd Bacon.* Sp: D. D. Beauchamp, William Bowers and Richard Flournoy, b/o story by Beauchamp ("Enough For Happiness"). Cast: Jean Simmons, Arthur Hunnicutt, Edgar Buchanan, Wallace Ford, Raymond Walburn, Jimmy Hunt, Ralph Dumke, Hope Landin, Gus Shilling.

47. RIVER OF NO RETURN. 20th Century-Fox, 1954 (c). *Otto Preminger.* Sp: Frank Fenton. Cast: Marilyn Monroe, Rory Calhoun, Tommy Rettig, Douglas Spencer, Edward Hinton, Murvyn Vye.

48. TRACK OF THE CAT. Warner Bros., 1954 (c). *William A. Wellman.* Sp: A. I. Bezzerides, b/o novel by Walter Van Tilburg Clark. Cast: Teresa Wright, Tab Hunter, Diana Lynn, Beulah Bondi, Philip Tonge, Carl Switzer.

49. NOT AS A STRANGER. United Artists, 1955. *Stanley Kramer.* Sp: Edward and Edna Anhalt, b/o novel by Morton Thompson. Cast: Olivia de Havilland, Frank Sinatra, Gloria Grahame, Broderick Crawford, Charles Bickford, Myron McCormick, Lon Chaney, Jesse White, Harry Morgan, Lee Marvin.

50. THE NIGHT OF THE HUNTER. United Artists, 1955. *Charles Laughton.* Sp: James Agee, b/o novel by Davis Grubb. Cast: Shelley Winters, Lillian Gish, Evelyn Varden, Peter Graves, Billy Chapin, Sally Jane Bruce, James Gleason.

51. MAN WITH THE GUN. United Artists, 1955. *Richard Wilson.* Sp: Richard Wilson and N. B. Stone, Jr. Cast: Jan Sterling, Karen Sharpe, Henry Hull, Emile Meyer, John Lupton, Barbara Lawrence, Ted De Corsia, Angie Dickinson.

52. FOREIGN INTRIGUE. United Artists, 1956 (c). *Sheldon Reynolds.* Sp: Sheldon Reynolds. Cast: Genevieve Page, Ingrid Thulin, Frederick O'Brady, Gene Decker, Inga Tidblad, John Padovano, Frederick Schrecker.

53. BANDIDO. United Artists, 1956 (c). *Richard Fleischer.* Sp: Earl Felton. Cast: Ursula Theiss, Gilbert Roland, Zachary Scott, Rodolfo Acosta, Henry Brandon, Douglas Fowley, Jose I. Torvay, Victor Junco.

54. HEAVEN KNOWS, MR. ALLISON. 20th Century-Fox, 1957 (c). *John Huston.* Sp: John Lee Mahin and John Huston, b/o novel by Charles Shaw. Cast: Deborah Kerr.

55. FIRE DOWN BELOW. Columbia, 1957 (c). *Robert Parrish*. Sp: Irwin Shaw, b/o novel by Max Catto. Cast: Rita Hayworth, Jack Lemmon, Herbert Lom, Bernard Lee, Bonar Colleano, Edric Conner, Peter Illing, John Miller, Anthony Newley, Eric Pohlmann.

56. THE ENEMY BELOW. 20th Century-Fox, 1957 (c). *Dick Powell*. Sp: Wendell Mayes, b/o novel by Commander D. A. Raynes. Cast: Curt Jurgens, Al Hedison, Theodore Bikel, Russell Collins, Kurt Kreuger.

57. THUNDER ROAD. United Artists, 1958. *Arthur Ripley*. Sp: James Atlee Phillips and Walter Wise, b/o story by Robert Mitchum. Cast: Gene Barry, Jacques Aubuchon, Keely Smith, Trevor Bardette, Sandra Knight, Jim Mitchum, Betsy Holt, Francis Kroon, Randy Sparks.

58. THE HUNTERS. 20th Century-Fox, 1958 (c). *Dick Powell*. Sp: Wendell Mayes, b/o novel by James Salter. Cast: Robert Wagner, Richard Egan, May Britt, John Gabriel, Lee Philips.

59. THE ANGRY HILLS. MGM, 1959. *Robert Aldrich*. Sp: A.I. Bezzerides, b/o novel by Leon Uris. Cast: Elisabeth Mueller, Stanley Baker, Gia Scala, Theodore Bikel, Sebastian Cabot, Peter Illing.

60. THE WONDERFUL COUNTRY. United Artists, 1959 (c). *Robert Parrish*. Sp: Robert Ardrey, b/o novel by Tom Lea. Cast: Julie London, Gary Merrill, Pedro Armendariz, Jack Oakie, Albert Dekker, Charles McGraw, Satchel Paige, Victor Mendoza.

61. HOME FROM THE HILL. MGM, 1960 (c). *Vincente Minnelli*. Sp: Harriet Frank, Jr. and Irving Ravetch, b/o novel by William Humphrey. Cast: Eleanor Parker, George Peppard, George Hamilton, Everett Sloane, Luana Patten, Anne Seymour, Constance Ford.

62. THE NIGHT FIGHTERS. United Artists, 1960. *Tay Garnett*. Sp: Robert Wright Campbell, b/o novel by Arthur Roth *(A Terrible Beauty)*. Cast: Anne Heywood, Dan O'Herlihy, Cyril Cusack, Richard Harris, Marianne Benet, Niall MacGinnis, Harry Brogan, Eileen Crowe.

63. THE GRASS IS GREENER. Universal-International, 1960 (c). *Stanley Donen*. Sp: Hugh and Margaret Williams, b/o their play. Cast: Cary Grant, Deborah Kerr, Jean Simmons, Moray Watson.

64. THE SUNDOWNERS. Warner Brothers, 1960 (c). *Fred Zinnemann*. Sp: Isobel Lennart, b/o novel by Jon Cleary. Cast: Deborah Kerr, Peter Ustinov, Glynis Johns, Dina Merrill, Chips Rafferty, Michael Anderson, Jr., Lola Brooks, Wylie Watson.

65.   THE LAST TIME I SAW ARCHIE. United Artists, 1961. *Jack Webb.*
Sp: William Bowers. Cast: Jack Webb, Martha Hyer, France Nuyen, Joe Flynn,
James Lydon, Del Moore, Louis Nye, Richard Arlen, Don Knotts, Robert
Strauss, Harvey Lembeck.

66.   CAPE FEAR. Universal-International, 1962. *J. Lee Thompson.* Sp: James
R. Webb, b/o novel by John D. MacDonald *(The Executioners).* Cast: Gregory
Peck, Polly Bergen, Lori Martin, Martin Balsam, Jack Kruschen, Telly Savalas,
Barrie Chase.

67.   THE LONGEST DAY. 20th Century-Fox, 1962. *Andrew Marton, Ken
Annakin, Bernhard Wicki.* Sp: Cornelius Ryan, Romain Gary, James Jones,
David Pursall and Jack Seddon. Cast: John Wayne, Richard Burton, Rod
Steiger, Henry Fonda, Red Buttons, Robert Ryan, Sean Connery, Jean-Louis
Barrault.

68.   TWO FOR THE SEESAW. United Artists, 1962. *Robert Wise.* Sp: Isobel
Lennart, b/o play by William Gibson. Cast: Shirley MacLaine, Edmond Ryan,
Elisabeth Fraser, Eddie Firestone, Billy Gray.

69.   THE LIST OF ADRIAN MESSENGER. Universal-International, 1963.
*John Huston.* Sp: Anthony Veiller, b/o story by Philip MacDonald. Cast:
George C. Scott, Dana Wynter, Clive Brook, Kirk Douglas, Frank Sinatra, Burt
Lancaster, Tony Curtis.

70.   RAMPAGE. Warner Brothers, 1963 (c). *Phil Karlson.* Sp: Robert I. Holt
and Marguerite Roberts, b/o novel by Alan Caillou. Cast: Elsa Martinelli, Jack
Hawkins, Sabu, Cely Carrillo, Emile Genest, Stephan Schnabel.

71.   MAN IN THE MIDDLE. 20th Century-Fox, 1964. *Guy Hamilton.* Sp:
Keith Waterhouse and Willis Hall, b/o novel by Howard Fast *(The Winston
Affair).* Cast: France Nuyen, Barry Sullivan, Trevor Howard, Keenan Wynn,
Sam Wanamaker, Alexander Knox, Gary Cockrell.

72.   WHAT A WAY TO GO! 20th Century-Fox, 1964 (c). *J. Lee Thompson.*
Sp: Betty Comden and Adolph Green, b/o story by Gwen Davis. Cast: Shirley
MacLaine, Paul Newman, Dean Martin, Dick Van Dyke, Gene Kelly, Robert
Cummings.

73.   MISTER MOSES. United Artists, 1965 (c). *Ronald Neame.* Sp: Charles
Beaumont and Monja Danischewsky, b/o novel by Max Catto. Cast: Carroll
Baker, Alexander Knox, Ian Bannen, Raymond St. Jacques.

74.  THE WAY WEST. United Artists, 1967 (c). *Andrew V. McLaglen.* Sp: Ben Maddow and Mitch Lindemann, b/o novel by A.B. Guthrie. Cast: Kirk Douglas, Richard Widmark, Lola Albright, Michael Witney, Stubby Kaye.

75.  EL DORADO. Paramount, 1967 (c). *Howard Hawks.* Sp: Leigh Brackett, b/o novel by Harry Brown *(The Stars in Their Courses).* Cast: John Wayne, James Caan, Charlene Holt, Arthur Hunnicutt, Paul Fix, Christopher George.

76.  ANZIO. Columbia, 1967 (c). *Edward Dmytryk.* Sp: Harry Craig, b/o novel by Wynford Vaughan-Thomas. Cast: Peter Falk, Earl Holliman, Mark Damon, Arthur Kennedy, Robert Ryan.

77.  VILLA RIDES. Paramount, 1968 (c). *Buzz Kulik.* Sp: Robert Towne and Sam Peckinpah. Cast: Yul Brynner, Charles Bronson, Grazia Buccella, Herbert Lom, Robert Viharo, Frank Wolff.

78.  5 CARD STUD. Paramount, 1968 (c). *Henry Hathaway.* Sp: Marguerite Roberts, b/o novel by Ray Gaulden. Cast: Dean Martin, Inger Stevens, Roddy McDowall, Katherine Justice, John Anderson.

79.  SECRET CEREMONY. Universal, 1969 (c). *Joseph Losey.* Sp: George Tabori. Cast: Elizabeth Taylor, Mia Farrow, Pamela Brown, Peggy Ashcroft.

80.  YOUNG BILLY YOUNG. United Artists, 1969 (c). *Burt Kennedy.* Sp: Will Henry. Cast: Angie Dickinson, Robert Walker, David Carradine, Jack Kelly, John Anderson, Deana Martin.

81.  THE GOOD GUYS AND THE BAD GUYS. Warner Bros.–Seven Arts, 1969 (c). *Burt Kennedy.* Sp: Ronald M. Cohen and Dennis Shryack. Cast: George Kennedy, Martin Balsam, David Carradine, Tina Louise.

82.  RYAN'S DAUGHTER. MGM, 1970 (c). *David Lean.* Sp: Robert Bolt. Cast: Trevor Howard, Sarah Miles, Christopher Jones, John Mills, Leo McKern, Barry Foster.

83.  GOING HOME. MGM, 1972 (c). *Herbert B. Leonard.* Sp: Lawrence B. Marcus. Cast: Brenda Vaccaro, Jan-Michael Vincent, Lou Gilbert.

84.  THE WRATH OF GOD. MGM, 1972 (c). *Ralph Nelson.* Sp: Ralph Nelson. Cast: Victor Buono, Rita Hayworth, Paula Pritchett, Frank Langella, John Colicos.

85.   THE FRIENDS OF EDDIE COYLE. Paramount, 1973 (c). *Peter Yates*. Sp: Paul Monash, b/o novel by George V. Higgins. Cast: Peter Boyle, Richard Jordan, Steven Keats, Alex Rocco, Mitchell Ryan.

86.   THE YAKUZA. Warner Bros.–Seven Arts, 1975 (c). *Sydney Pollack*. Sp: Robert Towne and Paul Schrader, b/o story by Leonard Schrader. Cast: Brian Keith, Takakura Ken, Herb Edelman, Richard Jordan, Kishi Keiko, James Shigeta.

87.   FAREWELL, MY LOVELY. Avco Embassey, 1975 (c). *Dick Richards*. Sp. David Zelag Goodman, b/o novel by Raymond Chandler. Cast: Charlotte Rampling, John Ireland, Sylvia Miles, Jack O'Halloran, Anthony Zerbe, Harry Dean Stanton. Also filmed in 1942 as *The Falcon Takes Over* and in 1945 as *Murder, My Sweet*.

# INDEX

## ABOUT THE AUTHOR

John Belton has written film reviews for *The Village Voice* and *Rolling Stone*. His articles have appeared in *The Velvet Light Trap*, *The Silent Picture*, *Monogram*, *Cinema*, *Film Quarterly*, and *Film Heritage*. He is the author of *The Hollywood Professionals*, vol. 3 (Tantivy/Barnes) and has taught film at Harvard University, The Orson Welles Film School, and Brooklyn College.

## ABOUT THE EDITOR

Ted Sennett is the author of *Warner Brothers Presents*, a tribute to the great Warners films of the thirties and forties, and of *Lunatics and Lovers*, on the long-vanished but well-remembered "screwball" comedies of the past. He is also the editor of *The Movie Buff's Book* and has written about films for magazines and newspapers. He lives in New Jersey with his wife and three children.